THE
MARJAEYA
A CANDID CONVERSATION

HIS EMINENCE

GRAND AYATOLLAH
SAYYID M.S. ALHAKEEM

TRANSLATED BY JALAL MOUGHANIA

Author: Grand Ayatollah Sayyid Muhammad Saeed Al-Hakeem

Translated by: Jalal Moughania

Printed in the United States.

ISBN: 978-1943393800

To the men of vision, foresight, and judgment whose sacrifices preserved the faith of our Grand Prophet Muhammad (s)

CONTENTS

ABOUT THE AUTHOR

His Eminence Grand Ayatollah Sayyid Muhammad Saeed Al-Hakeem was born in the Holy City of Najaf in 1934 CE. His father, Ayatollah Sayyid Muhammad Ali Al-Hakeem, was a prominent scholar of his time. The author grew under the tutelage of his father, who began to teach him the basic courses of Islamic sciences before the age of ten.

Since his youth, His Eminence was known for his knowledge, ethics, and piety. He was respected amongst his peers and teachers for his keen understanding of the religious sciences and critical approach in discussion. He was always alongside his father in the gatherings of scholarly learning and intellectual discourse.

Grand Ayatollah Sayyid Muhammad Saeed Al-Hakeem was given special attention by his maternal grandfather Grand Ayatollah Sayyid Muhsen Al-Hakeem, who assigned his grandson the task of referencing the manuscripts of his well renowned jurisprudential encyclopedia *Mustamsak Al-'Urwa Al-Wuthqa*. In the course of reviewing the manuscripts, His Eminence would discuss the text with his grandfather.

Through those sessions he gained a great wealth of knowledge and showcased his understanding and skill in the Islamic sciences.

During his time at the Islamic Seminary of Najaf, His Eminence studied under some of the most prominent scholars. Those scholars included his father, his maternal grandfather, Grand Ayatollah Sheikh Hussain Al-Hilli, and Grand Ayatollah Sayyid Abulqasim Al-Khoei.

At the age of thirty-four, after having spent more than two decades of his life in the pursuit of religious learning, he began offering *bahth kharij* (advanced seminars) in the principles of jurisprudence. Two years later, he began offering advanced seminars in jurisprudence based on the books of Al-Sheikh Al-A'dham Murtadha Al-Ansari and his grandfather Grand Ayatollah Sayyid Muhsen Al-Hakeem. Since then, His Eminence would continue to teach advanced seminars despite the challenges and obstacles he would face.

Along with his teachers and peers, the Grand Ayatollah was active in public affairs ever since he joined the seminary. He was amongst the group of scholars that supported Grand Ayatollah Sayyid Muhsen Al-Hakeem in his movement against communist influence in Iraq. In 1963, Grand Ayatollah Sayyid Muhammad Saeed Al-Hakeem signed the notable petition from the seminary that denounced President Abdul Salam Arif's attempt to impose communism in Iraq.

When the Baathist regime overthrew its predecessor and took control of Iraq, Grand Ayatollah Al-Hakeem continued his activism against the state's dictatorial policies. Most notably, he would defy Baathist threats to execute anyone who would fulfill the ritual of walking toward the city of Karbala as a commemoration of the sacrifices made there fourteen centuries ago. Due to this defiance, the Grand Ayatollah became a pursued target of the Baathist regime and was forced into hiding until the regime finally closed the case. Yet despite all the harassment and persecution, Grand Ayatollah Al-Hakeem remained in Najaf and refused to join the escape away from Baathist tyranny. He saw the mass departure as a threat to the existence of Najaf's seminary, and so decided to stay in the city to ensure its continuity.

On May 9th, 1983, after the Hakeem family's refusal to support the Baathist regime during the Iran-Iraq war, many of the family's members were arrested, including the Sayyid himself. There, they faced constant interrogation and all kinds of torture. They were beaten with nightsticks and attacked with electric shocks, along with other torture methods. With no access to any medical assistance, disease and illness began to spread. Still, the family's fortitude was not broken and they persevered.

Shortly after the mass imprisonment of the family, the Grand Ayatollah began offering classes in Quranic exegesis. He found no other books or sources for study in the Baathist prison system other than a worn copy of the Holy Quran. The wardens soon found out about his class and forced him to stop teaching. Nonetheless, religious discussions and commemorations continued in secrecy throughout their years of imprisonment. During those years, a total of sixteen members of the Hakeem family were executed by the regime.

In 1985, the remainder of the imprisoned members of the Hakeem family was moved to Abu Ghraib prison, which was a minimum-security prison at the time. There, the Grand Ayatollah found an opportunity to continue teaching the advanced seminars he had offered before imprisonment. Since most of the inmates with him were highly educated seminarians and students of his, he quickly seized the opportunity to expand on an educational curriculum.

Finally, on June 7, 1991, His Eminence and the remainder of the Hakeem family were released from prison. However, that did not mean an end to Baathist harassment. The Baathist authorities harassed him in an attempt to have him accept the title of an official "state designated religious authority." He definitively refused such offers, asserting that religious authority is and must always be independent. Due to his firm position, the Iraqi government imposed significant restrictions on the Grand Ayatollah. Amongst those restraints included a ban on publishing any of his books and scholarly work and broad restrictions on his travel.

After the passing of Grand Ayatollah Sayyid Abulqasim Al-Khoei the following year, many scholars and seminarians petitioned Grand Ayatollah Al-Hakeem to assume the obligations and duties of a Marja' – the religious authority to whom the believers refer to in issues of law. In compliance with the repeated petitions of students and peers, he put forward his views on Islamic law and practice, thus becoming one of the

most prominent religious authorities of the time. He continued his scholarly work, writing and teaching across the fields
of Islamic sciences. Currently based in the Holy City of Najaf,
Grand Ayatollah M.S. Al-Hakeem is one of the leading
worldwide contemporary religious authorities for Shia Ithna
Asheri Muslims.

TRANSLATOR'S PREFACE

Discourse on the topic of *Marjaeya* is a frequent topic between practicing Muslims. It is also a subject of intrigue to non-Muslims who are interested in learning more about the source of guidance for Shia Muslims. Nonetheless, greater focus on these discussions have been by Muslims themselves, particularly Shia Muslims. The original Arabic publication of Grand Ayatollah Sayyid Saeed Al-Hakeem, *Al-Marjaeya wa Qadaya Ukhra*, served as an excellent overview of the most pressing issues on the topic.

The original publication is the result of a candid discussion on matters pertaining to the *Marjaeya* from a series of questions offered to Sayyid Al-Hakeem. The Grand Ayatollah provided comprehensive answers to those critical inquiries as a way to address people's questions and concerns on the subject. As we worked through reading, studying, and translating the work we could see the genuineness, prudence, and pragmatism of the Grand Ayatollah.

A constant theme was found throughout the work – *ibra' al-thimma* – relieving one's duty before God. Everything that the jurists do is based on this concept. The actions they take and the decisions they make are driven by that motivation to have a clear conscience and ensure that their burden before God is relieved, and that they can stand on the Day of Judgment before God and know that they did everything they could to arrive at truth and guide people as such.

Working on this translation allowed us to gain an even greater appreciation for the Marjaeya. We were able to deepen our own understanding of the principles at stake and the driving forces that guide this leadership to guide others. Sayyid Al-Hakeem's wisdom and selflessness in the topic was evident throughout his writing. Although clearly he is a religious authority himself, he focused his work on the experiences and leadership of those who came before him. The Grand Ayatollah emphasized the lessons and values exemplified by our late scholars and jurists. It is one thing to hear read answers from a scholar who is speaking about the Marjaeya generally; it is an entirely different experience to receive the answer directly from the Marja himself.

Having the honor and privilege to work on this was both humbling and rewarding. We were humbled by the humility of the Grand Ayatollah, as well as his deep care and concern for the wellbeing of all people. We felt rewarded by the knowledge and insight we gained in studying and translating this work. We especially feel rewarded in realizing how this work could be of such great benefit to our English-speaking communities living in North America, Europe, and elsewhere in the world.

In order to realize the gravity of undertaking such work, one would have to understand the great intellectual and spiritual heritage of Grand Ayatollah Al-Hakeem. Not only is Sayyid Al-Hakeem one of the leading jurists of his time, he comes from a rich heritage of scholarship and leadership. He is the grandson of Grand Ayatollah Sayyid Muhsen Al-Hakeem who was the undisputed leading jurist of his time, known as *Marja' Al-Ta'ifa.*

Having survived the torture of eight years of imprisonment under the Baathist regime, and the execution of over sixty family members, Sayyid Al-Hakeem refused to leave Najaf. Grand Ayatollah Al-Hakeem insisted that if the scholars of Najaf did not remain in the city the heritage of the great seminary would be lost. By staying, he ensured that he would sit at the vanguard of protecting the seminary against the challenges and obstacles it would face throughout the decades.

There were definitely challenges in translating this work. First, we must admit the great difficulty that comes with attempting to translate verses from the Holy Quran, often cited by the Grand Ayatollah. Muslim scholars have pondered on the meanings of the holy text for centuries, and the meanings of its verses only grow deeper as time passes. The process of translation always requires us to find precise meanings for the passages that we translate. However, when we encounter the majesty of the Holy Quran, we find ourselves incapable of fully understanding, let alone properly translating, its true and deep meanings. Accordingly, we turned to the works of translators who have attempted to do this before. Although no translation can do justice to the Holy Quran, we found that the translation of Ali Quli Qarai to be proper in understanding when compared to the understanding of the text as derived by our grand scholars. As such, we decided to rely on Qarai's translations throughout this book, with some adaptations that allowed us to weave the verses more properly with the rest of the work.

A second great limitation came with translation of the narrations of the Grand Prophet Muhammad (s) and his Holy Household (a). Their words contain immense meaning and spiritual power. We attempted to convey these passages to the reader in a tone that is understandable without deviating from the essence of the words of these divine personalities. We pray that we were successful in this endeavor.

Finally, we would like to acknowledge the individuals without whom this work would not have been possible. First, we must thank Grand Ayatollah Al-Hakeem for his guidance and leadership, in addition to his blessing with this work. We must also thank Sayyid Riyadh Al-Hakeem and Sayyid Muhammad Hussain Al-Hakeem, who were instrumental during the process of writing and publishing this book.

Most importantly, we thank the Almighty for granting us such a unique opportunity and allowing us the tremendous honor to be able to partake in this project.

Sincerely,

Jalal Moughania

The Mainstay Foundation

INTRODUCTION

The Shia Twelver school of thought has distinguished itself by keeping the gates of *ijtihad* – expert deduction of religious law – open throughout the passage of time. Its scholars have thus committed to this; they have not intended in practicing *ijtihad* to expand their scope of influence, or to change laws based on the changing of circumstances and times, or to appease the masses or the rulers and those who hold power. Instead, *ijtihad* to them is exerting their utmost effort and ability to know the religious law by examining its original sources. These scholars have sought to protect it and safeguard it as a trust given to them by God, one that He will question them about when they stand before Him on the Day of Judgment.

In the same way, the Shia Twelver school of thought has distinguished itself through emulation (*taqleed*) – the act of returning to the trusted jurist, who does not compromise in matters of worship and transactions, by exerting efforts in research and review in this field. The jurist is a guardian over the religious rulings, and does not lack in research or inquiry. In the Shia school, the jurist does not seek to appease rulers or the masses through his work. The jurist does not seek fame or popularity by innovating new rules, by simply making things easier for people, or by lessening their religious obligations to gain their favor. Nor does the jurist do anything of the like for personal gain. The jurist avoids these actions in fear of God and His displeasure and punishment. Accordingly, it is commonly seen that the people give the utmost respect and honor to the jurists in general, and to the jurist they do *taqleed* of in particular, because of their earnest approach to their scholarly work.

The Shia Twelver school of thought has the distinct right to lift its head high with pride and honor for its diligence in safeguarding the laws of God. It has placed the utmost importance in deriving the law from its original sources, remained resilient against the test of time, and endured oppression and sedition throughout.

All of this was done with the grace of the sincere and dedicated scholars – against whom none can make any valid accusation before God – and the believing men and women who followed them and take their faith only from those who are fit to safeguard the religion and its sanctity. The believers do not take their faith from those who do not possess the traits of trustworthiness and piety, and are careless to the paths they embark, and place themselves in situations of suspicion and doubt. In this regard, the believers keep the teachings of the Imams of the Holy Household at the forefront of their minds, which stand in compliance with the rulings of sound mind, the Holy Book, and the Prophetic Tradition.

Much has been narrated from the Infallibles (a) in this regard, amongst which is what has been relayed from Imam Ja'far Al-Sadiq (a) who said, after disparaging those that had blindly followed their unqualified clergy:

> *As for those amongst the jurists who safeguard their selves, preserve their faith, oppose their whims, obey the order of their Master, then the people may follow them. That would be only some of the jurists of the Shia, not all of them. As for those who rode the ships of immorality and indecency... do not accept anything they claim to relay on our behalf.*

It is a requirement for the believers, both the scholars and followers amongst them, to know the grand responsibility that has been set upon their shoulders, and the weight of what God has entrusted them with. Let it be known that the first and last concern for the scholar is to know the truth and to protect it. It is to ascertain the religious rulings from their original sources, and to proclaim it, fulfilling one's religious duty without caring for the number of followers or supporters they have, nor for showing off or ostentation, nor for other worldly pursuits which fade away and Satanic destructive invitations. At the forefront of the believer's eyes are the words of God, "Had he faked any sayings in Our name, We would have surely seized him by the right hand and then cut off his aorta, and none of you could have held Us off from him."[1]

---

[1] The Holy Quran, 69:44-47.

Similarly, the concern of the followers should be to fulfill their duties in following the religious laws, by obtaining them from the scholars who act according to their knowledge – from the people of wisdom, piety, integrity, sincerity, and uprightness. These jurists are the people with such impeccable character, they are immune from allegations and cannot be chewed by whimsical discussions. This is due to their distance from situations of suspicion and misgivings, with complete ascertainment and deliberation. As such, the followers can then have the foresight to see themselves cleared from any liability and be excused before God, on that Day in which everything is presented before Him and nothing will be hidden. Their following of a person should not be founded upon haste or the deception of flashy words or his concordance with their whims and desires. It is God who watches over them. He is the overseer of all the secrets and knows of all the subtleties and all that is in the conscience. Nothing as small as an atom, be it in the heavens or on Earth, can ever possibly escape Him.

People may be confused, due to particular circumstances or pressing situations, before the numerous claims and multiplicity of trends. That, however, should not be an excuse for negligence and dereliction in fulfilling one's duty. Thus, no matter how much the circumstances and seditions cause confusion, God will never abandon His proof on Earth nor will the teachings of His religion be hidden from those who seek it earnestly.

As for those who strive in Us, We shall surely guide them in Our ways, and God is indeed with the virtuous.[2] *Say, 'To God belongs the conclusive argument. Had He wished, He would have surely guided you all.'*[3]

Praise be to God, Lord of the Worlds.

---

[2] The Holy Quran, 29:69.
[3] The Holy Quran, 6:149.

TAQLEED

FOLLOWING THE SCHOLARS SINCE THE FIRST ERA

Was emulation (taqleed), and following the scholars,
existent amongst the followers of the Holy Household
(a) during the times of the Imams (a) or during the
minor occultation, or did it begin afterwards?

All praise is due to God the Lord of the Worlds. Peace and
blessings be upon our master and prophet Muhammad (s)
and upon his Holy Household.

Referring to the scholars and asking them for practical religious rulings has been the practice of the Shias and all Muslims since the first era of Islam. In every age there were a
group of people that were responsible for providing the religious rulings. The textual sources have mentioned the undertaking of some Shia scholars of such a task. An example of
such scholars was Aban ibn Taghleb, whom Shaykh Al-Tusi
praised and said in his regard, "[Imam] Al-Baqir (a) said to

him, 'Sit in the Mosque of Medina, and give rulings to the people, for I love to see amongst my followers the likes of you.' Thus, he sat."[1]

Ma'adh ibn Muslim Al-Nahwi is another example. He narrates his conversation with Imam Al-Sadiq (a):

> He said, 'I was told that you sit in the mosque and give rulings to the people.'
> I said, 'Yes, and I wanted to ask you about this before I leave. I sit in the mosque and a man comes to me asking about a certain matter. If I know that he is in opposition to you I answer him based on what they do. When a man comes, and I know that he is an admirer and a follower of yours, I answer him based on what has been relayed from you. When a man comes whom I don't know, and I have no knowledge of who he is, I say to him, 'It has been relayed from this person as this and from the other person as that...' and so I include your position amongst those.'
> The Imam said to me, 'Do as such, for that is what I do.[2]

However, Shia jurisprudence did not stand out by itself or through its jurists in the first era, due to the seditions and tragedies endured by the Shia. This was the reason for the Shia's attention to the political dimension of the time and their focus on having the Holy Household assume power and take the helm, without the people knowing the details of the jurisprudential differences between the Holy Household and

---

[1] Al-Tusi, *Al-Fihrist*, 17.
[2] Al-Amili, *Wasa'il Al-Shia*, 18:108.

the others. They may have even sought and taken the religious rulings from those outside of the school of thought, unaware of their contradiction to the rulings of the Holy Household in those matters.

After the tragedy of Karbala – when the hope that the Holy Household would take over political authority in the near future was diminished. Through the telling of the tale of their tragedy, their rights became apparent and so did the injustice and deviance of the opposing side. Accordingly, the followers of the Holy Household gravitated towards them in order to receive guidance in their religion in the matters of theology and jurisprudence, and they departed from others and rejected them.

The Imams (a) saw the fertile ground and the right opportunity to focus on their followers' understanding of their teachings in theology, jurisprudence, and the measures of love, hate, allegiance, and aversion. They strived in establishing an educational institution that would hold those teachings and spread them to their followers, so that they would be in no need to refer to others.

Imam Al-Baqir's (a) attention to this matter is apparent in his will to his son Imam Al-Sadiq (a). In a verified narration from Imam Al-Sadiq (a) he says,

> *When my father was passing away he said to me, 'O Ja'far, I charge you with good toward my companions.'*

I said, 'May I be sacrificed for you! By God, I will leave them in such a state that wherever an individual amongst them may be, he will have no need to ask anyone.[3]

He fulfilled that promise. The Shia began seeking their scholars and referring to them. Amongst them rose a group that would give the religious rulings, just as the Imams (a) advised them.

In a verified narration by Shu'ayb Al-Aqarqoufi he states,

I said to Imam Al-Sadiq (a), 'Sometimes, we may need to ask about a certain matter, so who should we ask? He replied, 'You must go to [Abu Baseer] Al-Asadi.'[4]

And in another verified narration by Abdallah ibn Abi Ya'four he narrates,

I said to Imam Al-Sadiq (a), 'It is not all the time that I can see you, and coming to you is not [always] possible, and [so what if] a man from amongst our companions asks me of a matter and I don't have all that he asks for?' He said, 'What prevents you from Muhammad ibn Muslim Al-Thaqafi, for he heard [and narrated] from my father and he held a favorable position with him.'[5]

Ali ibn Al-Musayyab also narrates,

---

3 Al-Kulayni, *Al-Kafi*, 1:306.

4 Al-Toussi, *Ikhtiyar Ma'rifet Al-Rijal*, 1:400.

5 Al-Amili, *Wasa'il Al-Shia*, 18:105.

*I said to Imam Al-Rida (a), "My home is far away and I
am not able to reach you at all times, so from who should I
take my religious teachings from?'*

*He said, 'From Zakariya ibn Adam Al-Qummi, the one
who is trusted in his religious and worldly affairs.'*

*When I left, we went to Zakariya ibn Adam and I asked
him of those matters I needed [answers for].[6]*

And in a reliable narration by Abdul-Aziz ibn Al-Muhtadi,

*I asked Imam Al-Rida (a), 'I am not able to meet you at all
times, so from whom should I take my religious teachings?'*

He said, 'Take from Younus ibn Abdul-Rahman.[7]

It has also been relayed that the Imams (a) referred their followers to others – such as Al-Harith ibn Al-Mugheera, Zurara ibn A'yun, Al-Mufaddal ibn Umar, Al-'Amri and his son
– in narrations that are too numerous to recount fully here.[8]

Likewise, it has been relayed in many narrations that we are
to refer to our scholars generally without specification of any
particular person. One of such narrations is the famous
blessed instruction of the Awaited One, Imam Al-Mahdi
(may God hasten his reappearance), during the time of his
minor occultation: "In regards to the contemporary matters,
refer to the narrators of our tradition, for they are my proof

---

[6] Al-Amili, *Wasa'il Al-Shia*, 18:106.

[7] Al-Amili, *Wasa'il Al-Shia*, 18:107.

[8] Al-Kashi, *Al-Rijal*, 357, 483, 595; Al-Toussi, *Al-Rijal*, 509; and Al-Amili, *Wasa'il
Al-Shia*, 18:103-111.

upon you, and I am the proof of God."[9] Further such narrations have been relayed from Imam Al-Hadi (a) as well.

Therefore, the Shia's jurisprudence became comprehensive and thus they were in no need to refer to others outside the school of thought. In a reliable narration by Muhammad ibn Hakeem he states:

> *I said to Imam Al-Kadhim (a), 'May I be sacrificed for you! We have been given understanding of religion and God freed us from being in need of others, through you, such that if our people are in a gathering, there is no man who questions another except that the latter perceives the matter and presents the answer, by God's graces through you…*[10]

In a letter of Imam Al-Hadi (a) to Ahmad ibn Hatem and his brother he said,

> *Rely in your faith on those who have grown old in our love and who have a long history in adhering to our cause, for they are sufficient for you by God's will.*[11]

Furthermore, perhaps other people too referred back to them in predicaments, because they knew that they received their rulings from a pristine undiminishing source. In a trusted narration by Muhammad ibn Muslim he says,

> *I was sleeping one night on the rooftop when someone knocked on the door… I looked over and found a woman standing there.*

---

[9] Al-Amili, *Wasai'l Al-Shia*, 18:101.
[10] Al-Amili, *Wasai'l Al-Shia*, 18:61.
[11] Ibid, 18:110.

She said, 'My newlywed daughter was struck by the pangs of labor which did not desist until she died. But her baby still moves inside her. What do I do?' So I said, "O servant of God, [Imam] Muhammad ibn Ali ibn al-Hussain Al-Baqir (a) was asked about such a matter.

He said, 'The abdomen of the deceased is to be opened and the child is to be removed.' So do as such. O Servant of God, I am a private individual. Who directed you to me?'

She said, 'May God have mercy on you. I went to Abu Hanifa, the scholar of the school of opinionating. He said, 'I have no opinion with regards to this. But go to Muhammad ibn Muslim Al-Thaqafi, for he is an expert. Whatever religious ruling he gives you come back to me and let me know.'

I said, 'Go on in peace.'

The next day I went to the mosque and saw that Abu Hanifa was asking his companions about her. I then cleared my throat, and he said, 'God forgive us. Let us be."[12]

The Imams (a) emphasized the writing of their teachings and the narrations so that the knowledge may be preserved and people could benefit from it, especially in the age of occultation, when there would be no reference for people other than the books of narration. In a reliable narration by Abu Baseer he relates that he heard Imam Al-Sadiq (a) say, "Write, for you will not retain unless you write."[13]

---

[12] Al-Kashi, *Al-Rijal*, 146.

[13] Al-Amili, *Wasai'l Al-Shia*, 18:56.

In a trusted narration by Ubaid ibn Zurara, Imam Al-Sadiq (a) said, "Retain your writings, because you will soon be in need of them."[14]

Al-Mufaddal ibn Umar narrates that Imam Al-Sadiq (a) said,

> *Write and disseminate your knowledge amongst your brothers. Then, when you die, bequeath your books to your sons; for there will be a time of confusion that people will endure, whereby they will not find comfort in anything but their books.*[15]

Shia jurists began authoring books of religious rulings for people's reference, which would be most similar to today's *Risala Amaliya*.[16] An example of this that comes to mind is the book *Yawm w Layla* by Younus ibn Abdul-Rahman, a companion of Imam Al-Rida (a). There are numerous narrations from the Imams (a) that praise that work and assent to acting in accordance to it.[17]

Similar to this was a book *Yawm wa Layla*, also known as *Al-Ta'deeb*, by his student Ahmad ibn Abdullah ibn Mahran, who was also known as Ibn Khanba. Another was the treatise by Ali ibn Babawayh Al-Qummi, Shaykh Al-Sadouq's father, who passed away during the minor occultation. Other books were: *Al-Mutamassik bi-Habl Aal Al-Rasool* by Ibn Abi Aqeel

---

[14] Ibid.

[15] Ibid.

[16] Jurists that assume the position of Marja' traditionally publish their religious rulings in what is referred to as their "Risala Amaliya" – a practical guide to the Islamic laws. – Eds.

[17] Al-Amili, *Wasai'l Al-Shia*, 18:71-72.

Al-Ummani, who was also his contemporary, and *Al-Mukhtasar Al-Ahmadi fi Al-Fiqh Al-Muhammadi* by Ibn Al-Junayd, who lived in the same era.

The book *Men La Yahdharahu Al-Faqih,* written by Shaykh Al-Sadouq during the first period of the major occultation, was in fact a *risala amaliyya* that could be used by anyone that could not contact a jurist and ask him their questions. This book consisted of the religious edicts of Shaykh Al-Sadouq.

The works of the scholars continued one after the other, such as *Al-Muqni'a* by Shaykh Al-Mufid, *Jumal Al-'Ilm wa Al-'Amal* by Sayyid Al-Murtada, *Al-Nihaya fi Mujarrad Al-Fiqh wa Al-Fatawa* by Shaykh Al-Tousi, and many countless others.

THE IMPORTANCE OF DEFINING MARJAEYA AND TAQLEED

> *In the introduction to your Risala Amaliyya, you wrote an introduction regarding ijtihad and taqleed that was liked by many… what led you to that?*

It is too often that people mix their religious duties with habit or routine. People are led by their emotions and interests, which leads the duty-bound person to stray from upholding their religious responsibilities, becoming heedless to the reality of their situation. Some may even be stubborn in their pursuits, following their whims, making light of their obligations and rebelling against them. In such cases, such a discussion is needed as a warning for the heedless, and exhortation for the rebellious, and a shakeup to the conscience. God has said, "Admonish, for admonition indeed benefits the faithful."[18]

Similarly, such deviation could very well be a reason behind the efforts to distort the truth of *taqleed* and *marjaeya*. Many people do not have the ability to receive ideas from their original sources; instead they take it from observing its practical implementation. If the observed implementation falls outside of the true limitations of the matter concerned, it will likely distort the idea in the person's mind. This is especially relevant when the idea of *ijtihad* carries a much different meaning in the prevalent understanding that exists outside the Shia school of thought.

Through the introduction, we wished to show the true meaning of *ijtihad*, *taqleed*, and *marjayea* in the Shia school of thought, in its unclouded reality as provided by the clear legislative proofs and original sources.

In doing so, we uphold our duty in delivering the truth and defending the true *marjaeya*, that would otherwise be wronged due to the mistaken understanding of the concept.

---

[18] The Holy Quran, 51:55.

CONDITIONS OF THE MAJRA' TAQLEED

What are the fundamental conditions that a Marja'
must fulfill?

The fundamentals are *'adala* and *ijtihad* [and conditionally *a'lamiyya*].

By *'adala*, we mean the highest level of righteousness, which normally prevents a person from going against his religious duties or falling into even minor sins. If he is to, on the rare occasion, fall to the sin, he is quick to repent to God.

In regards to *ijtihad*, it is the ability to derive religious rulings and practical duties from the accepted sources of Islam, to the extent that one can stand before God with a clear conscience having upheld his duty. If an individual does not have this ability, then he lacks the requisite knowledge and it would be meaningless to refer to him and follow as a Marja.

These are the two fundamental conditions for a jurist to be followed.

Of course, when there are a number of jurists with conflicting views – as is the case today – we must give preference to the *a'lam*, or the most knowledgeable, amongst them. We have detailed this discussion in our research on jurisprudential matters,[19] As such, *a'lamiyya* becomes a third fundamental condition in following a Marja.

---

[19] Al-Hakeem, *Misbah Al-Minhaj*, Al-Ijtihad w Al-Taqleed, 67.

THE EFFECT OF PIETY IN THE MARJA' TAQLEED

Following up on your unique take on the 'adala of the Marja, in which you make it a condition that the Marja must have a high level of righteousness – at a level greater than the 'adala that an imam of congregational prayers must have – and considering what you have also mentioned that if two jurists are equal in their knowledge then one should follow the jurist that is greater in piety… so we ask what is the extent of the connection between strong piety and taqleed?

Our opinion regarding the *'adala* of the Marja comes from the idea that the greater a trust is, the greater the need there is for a trait that will ensure that the trust will not be mishandled. When our immaculate leadership entered occultation such that it was no longer able to directly deliver the teachings of God and ensure the fulfillment of religious obligations, there was no longer a safeguard against manipulation or loss of religious teachings or neglect of religious obligations. That is except for a high standard of righteousness and consciousness of God Almighty.

Therefore, the Marja is subject to the following challenges:

Firstly, he endures psychological pressure while deriving the law from the evidence before him. This is because evidence for rulings is not necessarily clear and the mind naturally leans toward the result that suits its presumptions, beliefs, and emotions. A jurist doing research may already be inclined towards a particular conclusion, clouded by his preconceived notions, and he will investigate the evidence and proof based on that. He may have acquired the ability to derive the Islamic laws such that he can validate the ruling that he derives, presenting what is not true proof as proof.

There is no barrier to stop him from manipulation, indulgence and being heedless in these matters, except the fear of God and His punishment, when he realizes that God is He who judges over us and nothing escapes Him, and that He cannot be fooled by loose justifications. It will then become clear to the jurist whether what he has determined to be proof is sufficient to stand against the standard of God's acceptance, and whether he is excused before Him. This God-consciousness is carried by him with the fullest usage of his abilities and the exertion of his utmost efforts, to pursue actual proofs, to arrive at them and to derive the laws based on them.

Secondly, the jurist faces external pressures in deriving the law. It is often the case that religious rulings, derived in accordance to the religious proofs, do not please the desires or interests of the ruling authorities or the general public, or are not in accordance with the present circumstances, or the overwhelming sentiments of the public.

The jurist may also be challenged with the ego. He may wish to be seen as an innovative thinker, or one who is distinguished above the others, or as a reformer and pioneer in modernism, or someone who is make things more convenient so that he may attract a greater following amongst the people. All of these pursuits push the jurist to try to free himself from the restraints of true evidence in deriving the religious rulings, to bypass them, and to adhere to unfounded justifications and excuses.

We see that some of the practitioners of those practical sciences – in which results of mistakes are often evident, such as medicine and engineering – fail to uphold their duty. This may be through negligence or purposefully for certain material motivations, even if it is mere laziness or boredom. Such an individual will bear the consequences of his actions, the least of which will be the manifestation of his error and failure in his work, sooner or later. The science of jurisprudence is quite different, however. Mistakes in jurisprudence cannot be seen outright by the general public. So how can one ensure against this if it was not for the jurists' highest level of God-fearing, piety and righteousness?

Thirdly, by the mere central role of the Marja he is subject to a number of religious challenges. He is tested with possession of monies and a position of prestige and authority amongst the people. This subjects him to the challenges of desire and the whispers of Satan. If he does not hold strong to caution and fear God, he will fall to his own doom and bring shame to the Marjaeya and religion.

All of these challenges call for the necessity of the Marja to be deeply religious, and to be pious, righteous and God-fearing to the highest degrees.

It is this premise that the followers of the Holy Household (a) have founded themselves upon and have come together with practical consensus, across the ages. And this is one of the strongest foundations of the Marjaeya, supported by the textual sources. The brilliant and radiant light of the Marjaeya comes from this.

Thus, you find that the Shia give their Maraje a high degree of sanctity. This would have been baseless if it were not for them believing them to be close to God through their piety, virtue, and upholding their noble duty in delivering God's laws to the people and bringing them closer to Him.

We ask God to make firm this nation on this clear path, and support it in all of its matters, and to protect it from deviance and the misguiding of seditions, for He is the most merciful and the guardian of the believers.

All this is in addition to the original condition of righteousness ('*adala*) of a high degree. As for the matter of preferring the more pious scholar when two jurists are equal in knowledge, this is based on a certain principle which does not permit giving the choice between two jurists who are equal in knowledge. But what we are certain of in that situation is that it is permissible to follow the most pious.

The details of this discussion, which we have discussed at length, can be referenced in the book, *Misbah Al-Minhaj*.

THE RATIONALE FOR TAQLEED

Some have posed the question of what warrants a person to refer back to the jurists and their jurisprudential research, when there is a possibility that the jurist does not derive what is the correct religious ruling in reality… what is your opinion on this subject?

There is no doubt that the error of jurists and loss of the actual religious ruling are the great trials of our faith. This tribulation came from the oppressors who usurped the rights of the Holy Household (a) and inevitably caused this situation of possible error in the religious rulings.

Given the reality of the circumstances, referring back to the jurists that meet all the necessary conditions is the only acceptable solution according to the Sharia. It is the only way to relieve the burden of one's duties before God, because the person would be relying on religious proofs that suffice to excuse a mistake or failure to arrive at the actual Islamic ruling.

This is the best solution for people, just as it is in all other matters and fields that we are dependent upon, and which are subject to error, such as medicine and engineering.

There is no alternative except two: either the complete suspension of the Sharia, by disregarding the religious rulings and ceasing to act upon them, or to take the religious rulings from sources not approved by the Sharia, such as uncertainties and conjectures which God has forbidden from acting upon, or the *ijtihad* of somebody who is unqualified to be followed. It is obvious that both of these alternatives are more dangerous than referring to the qualified jurists. Rational individuals would not accept either of them.

THE MOST
KNOWLEDGEABLE

Could you clarify the evidence behind the obligation in following the a'lam – the most knowledgeable jurist?

It is in the nature of a human being that if he needs to engage in a matter he is uninformed in, he refers to those who have knowledge in that field. That has been the course of people's lives in all things pertaining to this life and the afterlife, ranging from medicine and engineering to the sciences and disciplines of religion.

The verses of the Holy Quran and the noble traditions from the Ahlulbayt (a) direct us to turn to the scholars and jurists. One may then naturally suffice in referring to a scholar within his easy reach, without constricting himself in seeking the most knowledgeable.

But, if he realizes the existence of differences between scholars and the experts in their conclusions and on issues essential to him – as is the case in these times whereby the scholars present varying edicts in their books, which is the result of our historical distance from the age of the sources of legislation as well as the complexities of jurisprudential principles – then he will certainly pause and search about the true position amongst the various conclusions, for these differences go back to each scholar deeming the others to have been mistaken in their conclusions. In such a situation, what warrants a person to choose one scholar to follow over the others?

Prior to the occultation the Shia would go back to the Imams (a) whenever the scholars differed amongst themselves. This is because the word of the Imams (a) was the measure of what was right and wrong, what was truth and falsehood.

In a narration by Khayran the Servant he says,

> *I wrote to the [Imam (a)] asking whether or not to pray in clothes that have been touched by alcohol and pork? Our companions differed in the matter, some saying 'Pray in it, for God prohibited drinking it.' Others said, 'Don't pray in it.' He wrote back to me stating, 'Do not pray in it, for it is impure…'[1]*

Suma'a also narrates from Imam Al-Sadiq (a),

---

[1] Al-Amili, *Wasa'l Al-Shia*, 2:1017.

I asked him about a man who was confused between two other men from his faith with differing narrations on an issue. One of them says to act on the matter and the other says to refrain from it. What should he do? He replied, 'He is to postpone until he meets someone who will tell him of the correct verdict; he is at ease until then.'[2]

Yet, when ascertaining the truth becomes impossible due to the inability to go back to those whose words are conclusive – as is this case in our current era, the era of the occultation and tribulation – referring to the most knowledgeable is the logical predominant position that people rely on in all their affairs.

In our day-to-day affairs, when it comes to medicine, engineering, civil law and other matters, can a rational person rely on other than the most knowledgeable and abandon his words, when the experts differ? How so then with regards to the matter of religion which is tied to our bliss and salvation from eternal destruction? How is it possible to be negligent in it by following anyone who is not the most knowledgeable, in times of disagreement? What will our answer be when we meet God and stand before Him? Are God's commands lesser than matters of medicine, engineering, civil law, and other temporal fields, to forgo and be permissive with? This is enough evidence for a fair-minded person and a clear proof against those who are astray.

---

[2] Al-Amili, *Wasai'l Al-Shia*, 18:77.

A MISCONCEPTION

> *Some people postulate that it is not mandatory to fol-*
> *low the most knowledgeable jurist because the reli-*
> *gious rulings do not rise to that level of severity or*
> *importance. They draw the parallel to receiving treat-*
> *ment and advice from a physician on minor medical*
> *issues, whereby a person can go to any physician*
> *without needing to go to the foremost expert in the*
> *field. What are your thoughts on this?*

We do not know how such words have come from a believer!
The sanctity of the religious rulings is from the sanctity of
God, which He legislated, and for which we will be accounted
for. God says in reference to his most beloved creation, the
Seal of Prophets Muhammad (s),

> *Had he faked any sayings in Our name, We would have*
> *surely seized him by the right hand and then cut off his aorta,*
> *and none of you could have held Us off from him.*[3]

In a verified narration from Imam Al-Sadiq (a) following up
on a verdict given by Abu Hanifa he says, "From [his] verdict
and the likes of it, the sky would withhold its water and the
earth would withhold its blessings."[4]

---

[3] The Holy Quran, 69:44-47.
[4] Al-Amili, *Wasai'l Al-Shia*, 13:256.

In regards to referring back to any physician in the minor medical issues, this would be fine to people of reason in two situations.

Firstly, when the patient does not know about any differences that exist between the foremost expert and others in the field. He refers to any physician because of the simplicity of the matter, which is known by anyone in the field be it the most knowledgeable or not. A person in this situation is different from the matter at hand, because following the most knowledgeable is mandatory when there is knowledge of differences between the jurists in those religious rulings which are relevant to the person.

Secondly, when the patient cannot act in accordance to the edicts of the most knowledgeable, but can follow the edicts of one who is not. This is so long as there are no negative repercussions. For example, the foremost expert medical doctor prescribes a treatment that is extremely hard to attain, but the prescription by another doctor is easily accessible and will definitely not detriment the patient. The patient in this situation could use the second prescription, with the hope of receiving some benefit from it, while knowing himself to be safe from harm. In essence, it would be a form of precaution which is a virtue and definitely not forbidden.

This does not apply, however, with the religious rulings. They are of a nature that, to be attributed to God or acted upon in worship, require proof that would be sufficient on the Day of Judgment. Otherwise, the individual would be deserving of God's chastisement and liable for His punishment. Yes, there is no problem with following one who is not the most knowledgeable when his edict is more cautious, and is a virtue, as mentioned above.

To conclude this discussion we wish to give some more attention to a few issues.

Firstly, it appears from many of these questions – being of an educated inquisitive nature – that there is a particular focus given to these issues because of the prevailing public discourse on these subjects. These issues have busied scholars and experts, after research and scrutiny, in coming to detailed inferences within their studies and publications of many books.

Therefore, if the discussion taking place amongst the general public is undertaken by non-experts, then they should be advised of the very technical and scientific nature of these subjects. They cannot be addressed simply and superficially. Rather, it is like the rest of the sciences, like physics and chemistry, whereby the experts in those fields hold the scientific depth due to their many years of dedication and training. It is these individuals that are able to bring forth the proofs, the arguments, and the inferences in their fields, while grasping all the elements involved in such work.

So, if people are content with physicians, engineers, and experts in their sciences and arts, entrusting their lives, wealth and affairs to such individuals, why aren't people content with scholars of religion in their field? Are physicians and engineers more trustworthy in medicine and engineering than scholars are in religion? Are they more far removed from mistake and duplicity? Would a believer accept this characterization for himself?

If the discussion is undertaken by those who claim that they are experts, the obviousness of the religious evidence should be clearly apparent to them.

People must look into these matters with the experts of the field who are able to scrutinize the evidence before them to prove or disprove theories. Academic theories cannot be offered except after the experts have completed their research and scrutinization of the data and evidence before them.

It is not proper to shock the general believing community by such claims in a way that would suggest to them that these are legitimate reforms and solutions that the religious scholars are oblivious to, due to their "old ways" or "financial gain" or other similar suggestions. Such presumptive thoughts lead to reducing the people's trust in the scholars, as well as dismay and confusion amongst the believers.

It may be the perspective of whomever is making these claims that these solutions are not religiously derived to be shared with the experts so that they may research and scrutinize the evidence to check their validity. They may characterize them as "pragmatic solutions" dictated by the current state we live in, by which they attempt to avoid the negative repercussions they imagine are attached to any religiously derived solution. Thus, they try to convince the general public of these ideas to replace the religiously derived solutions that the scholars teach. If that is so, let these individuals come forth and clarify their perspective if they are true to their ideals. Thus, the believers will know what is being presented to them, whom they are dealing with, and what these individuals want of them.

Moreover, what is the purpose of this casting of doubt on the evidence of religious rulings and its relevance, and the obstinance with the fallacious rhetorical claims that are disguised as religious evidence? These ideas are as God says,

> ...*like a mirage in a plain, which the thirsty man supposes to be water. When he comes to it, he finds it to be nothing; but there he finds God, who will pay him his full account, and God is swift at reckoning.*[5]

Secondly, the pillars of Shia creed, history, and jurisprudence were established only through research and scrutiny. Shia scholars did not submit to them until they knew the opinions of the Immaculate Imams (a). They lived and spent over three centuries with them, during which the creed, its teachings, and its pillars were cemented. The Imams (a) did not leave until this foundation was established, upholding the necessary proof the community would need for its scholarship. It is not possible that the Immaculate Imams (a) would leave their followers without fulfilling God's complete proof upon them.

We do not impose our beliefs upon the believers for blind following; rather, all that we desire is that they are formidable

---

[5] The Holy Quran, 24:39.

when they come across such doubt-creation and rejection from some people, and that they try to search for the truth of the situation, by referring to the Holy Household (a), and to research from those who are trusted and pious. They should not be deceived into thinking that these people – the doubt-creators – do not speak except after they have done their research and diligence, out of having good faith in them, as such will lead to the neglection of religion and faith, the loss of which in this way has no excuse before God.

This is coupled with the narrations that have come from the Imams (a), that their cause on that day will be clearer than the light of the sun.[6]

This indicates to us that confusions from doubts and denials are indeed baseless and their falsehood is manifest to the person with insight. But they are seditions and betrayals, which God has promised in His words,

> *Do the people suppose that they will be let off because they say, 'We have faith,' and they will not be tested? Certainly We tested those who were before them. So God shall surely ascertain those who are truthful, and He shall surely ascertain the liars.*[7]

In another verse in the Holy Quran it is said that, "God will not leave the faithful in your present state, until He has separated the bad ones from the good."[8]

---

[6] Al-Kulayni, *Al-Kafi*, 1:336.

[7] The Holy Quran, 29:2-3.

[8] The Holy Quran, 3:179.

God has promised this to the Imams (a) especially in the time of occultation.

Mansour relays a conversation with Imam Al-Sadiq (a) where the Imam (a) said,

> O Mansour, this matter will not come to you until you are distinguished. No, by God, it will not come to you until you are tested. No, by God, it will not come to you until the wretched indulge in wretchedness and the good indulge in goodness.[9]

In a narration by Jabir Al-Ju'fi, he asks Imam Al-Baqir (a), "When will be your relief?" He replied, "Beware, beware. Our relief will not come until you are sieved, and then you are sieved, and then you are sieved –" he repeated that word three times, "– until God clears you of chagrin and only purity remains."[10]

Al-Mufaddal ibn Umar narrates that Imam Al-Sadiq (a) said,

> By God, your Imam will disappear for years during your age, so that you will be tested. And you will be thrashed just as the waves of the sea thrashes its sailing ships. None will be saved except those who God has taken an oath him.[11]

There are other narrations that speak to this truth, all emphasizing the necessity to prepare for these trials. One should be

---

[9] Al-Sadouq, *Kamal Al-Deen*, 334.
[10] Al-Toussi, *Al-Ghayba*, 206.
[11] Al-Kulayni, *Al-Kafi*, 1:336.

prepared and not be idle in his matters, for the consequences of idleness cannot be cured.

Thirdly, we hope that the believers (may God protect them) look at what we have mentioned with the insight, forethought, and reckoning that God has blessed us with and due to which He raised our ranks. It is through this intellect and forethought that God has delivered His proof upon us, and by way of it He rewards and He punishes

We hope that the believers will be wary of emotional and reactionary appeals that have no basis or foundation, but relies on the deception of hollow words, and the pleasantries of oratory and imagery, without having any foresight into the consequences of their actions.

The believers should be wary of baseless zeal and blind following, which can come about by being impressed by those making the claims, or being inclined to his line of thinking and becoming convinced due to it, without looking into the details. Such action may lead to misfortune and hardship beyond imagination.

The believers must know that the responsibility is immense; the judgment is severe; the judge is God. Nothing escapes Him and He has fulfilled His proof upon us.

DISTINGUISHING THE A'LAM

How do we distinguish the most knowledgeable from amongst the mujtahids[12] (jurists)?

Those who are personally incapable of undertaking the search must go back to the people of expertise.

Prior to the occultation, the Shia would often go back to the Imams (a) directly seeking the Imam's guidance on who they should refer to in matters of religion, just as we discussed previously.

However, during the occultation and our inability to refer back to the Imam (a), there is no better option than going back to the experts in this field – those who have reached a level of knowledge that enables them to evaluate and distinguish between the jurists. After reviewing their scientific theories in *usool*[13] and *fiqh*[14], their methodology in deduction, and their depth and extent of understanding of the proofs, it can become clear to the experts who is the most knowledgeable. In such a case, they are permitted to give testimony to who is the most knowledgeable (*a'lam*) and such testimony will be accepted.

---

[12] A mujtahid is a jurist who has the capabilities and qualifications to deduce the religious rulings from its sources. – Eds.

[13] *Usool al-fiqh*, or *usool* for short, refers to the study of the principles of jurisprudence – a science studied in the Islamic seminary alongside *fiqh* (jurisprudence). – Eds.

[14] *Fiqh* refers to the study of jurisprudence, and is a primary subject area studied in the Islamic seminary.

Of course, their testimony must be built on their comprehensive knowledge of the said jurists' opinions, scientific principles, deductive methods, and the like. Convictions and opinions are insufficient if they are not founded on such knowledge. In addition, such testimony must be based on knowledge of other non-scientific qualifications of a marja.

INTUITION IN SELECTING THE A'LAM

Is it permissible to rely on intuition in selecting who is the most knowledgeable jurist?

It is not permissible for a person to rely on his own intuition in following a jurist. It falls within the same category as following conjectures and acting on them, which has been clearly prohibited in the verses of the Holy Quran and the noble narrations. Intuition, on its own, does nothing in bringing one closer to the truth, unless it gets an individual to a state of certitude without doubt.

Likewise, it would not be permissible to rely on one's intuition – without investigating into the state of other jurists – in testifying to another person that the jurist he follows is the most knowledgeable. It is necessary in any testimony that it is borne out of certainty arising out of the perceptions of the senses direct practice. God says, "Were they witness to their creation? Their testimony will be written down and they shall be questioned."[15]

It is narrated that the Holy Prophet (s) said, "Do you see the sun? On such you should give your testimony or abstain [from giving it]."[16]

It is also narrated that Imam Al-Sadiq (a) said, "Do not testify to something until you know it like you know your own palm."[17]

Moreover, it is not permissible for someone else to rely on a testimony based on intuition, even if it is by one of the expert witnesses who claims to be certain and doubtless of his intuition. Rather, the authority of the testimony is contingent on sensory perception, as was discussed in further detail in the previous question.

SELECTING THE A'LAM BETWEEN CONFLICTING TESTIMONIES

> *The experts may differ in selecting who is the most knowledgeable jurist, where some experts advise people to follow one jurist and others advise to follow another. What should people do in that situation?*

---

[15] The Holy Quran, 43:19.

[16] Al-Amili, *Wasai'l Al-Shia*, 18:251.

[17] Ibid, 18:235.

If what is meant by the question is the personal responsibility of every person to uphold his religious duties and clear himself from any liability before God, then the instructions in the manuals of Islamic law deal with that.

What we have held is that if both parties of the experts fulfill the necessary conditions to be deemed to hold authority, the testimonies of both sides will fall away from holding authority, and the matter will be categorized as one in which the *a'lam* is indiscernible from amongst the jurists who are qualified to be followed in *taqleed*. While all the conditions of *taqleed* are fulfilled by all candidates – the most important being a high degree in *'adala* and piety – the duty-bound person should practice *ihtiyat* – which is to take the more precautionary edict between the two jurists – in order to ensure compliance with the Sharia, if it is possible.

However, if it is difficult to practice *ihtiyat* and it leads to hardships, the mercy of God allows us to do *taqleed* of one of them.

We need to ensure that we try our best to get as close as possible to the true religious ruling, and this means that one should choose to follow the jurist who is most likely to be *a'lam*, even if we cannot be absolutely certain of it. If the possibilities of either of the two being *a'lam* are equal, then the individual must choose the one who is more pious and precautious. If they are both equal in this respect too, then one may choose either one of them.

It is important to confirm these things, by seeking out pious and knowledgeable people of the community to clarify things as much as possible. Indeed, every individual is witness to himself, and God does not obligate a soul more than it can bear.

If the question here is about the stance that is taken regarding the variation in views, then the stance is quite natural given that the issue of identifying the most knowledgeable is one of reasoning and intuition. It is only natural that there would be differing views and opinions on the matter.

Differing perspectives should be treated with objectivity, openness, and mutual respect, especially given the fact that all sides are concerned with becoming closer to the truth as a form of protecting that which we have all been entrusted with and fulfilling our obligations. As the old saying goes, "Difference in opinion does not alter any aspect of love."

An individual should not force his own conviction on others. We lived through examples that can speak to this. The late Ayatollah Shaykh Muhammad Tahir Al-Shaykh Radhi was convinced with the idea of being able to choose between the late Sayyid Al-Hakeem[18] and Shaykh Aal Yaseen. There was

---

[18] The late Grand Ayatollah Sayyid Muhsin Al-Hakeem (d. 1390/1970) was known as "Marja Al-Ta'ifa" or the highest religious authority. His marjaeya was one of the most prominent and dynamic religious authorities of the century, given its activism and numerous projects. The late Sayyid Al-Hakeem was renowned for fighting the spread of communism in Iraq through his unwavering stances and famous verdict. He was greatly recognized for spreading awareness of the faith through social and community awareness programs, the Kufa University project, addressing crucial issues facing the nation head on, and his openness to all classes and groups of society.

a group of believers that frequently asked for his guidance and counsel in Khuzestan. He expressed his conviction in choosing any one of the two. They chose to follow Sayyid Al-Hakeem. The Shaykh chose for his family and relatives to follow Shaykh Aal Yaseen. All of the mentioned parties knew of Shaykh Radhi's position on this matter. Nonetheless, his relationships with his group and with the two Maraje remained in the best of terms.

Even before that time, Sayyid Al-Hakeem would advise people to follow the late Mirza Al-Na'eeni.[19] Meanwhile, his older brother Ayatollah Sayyid Mahmoud Al-Hakeem[20] would advise people to follow the late great jurist Shaykh Ali Al-Jawahiri.[21] Each of them advised people based on their own conviction, without affecting their strong relationships in any negative way. The history of our scholars is filled with such examples of wisdom, respect, and virtue.

---

[19] Shaykh Muhammad Hussain Al-Shaykh Abdelrahman Al-Na'eeni (1277 – 1355 AH) was one of the greats of the Islamic Seminary of Najaf. He was a Marja, a philosopher, a revolutionist in the Usooli tradition, and a leader in the revolution of his era.

[20] Sayyid Mahmoud Al-Sayyid Mahdi Al-Hakeem (1298 – 1375 AH) was of the great jurists and teachers of the Islamic Seminary of Najaf. He is notable for his commentary on many of the teaching texts for jurisprudence and principles of jurisprudence that are taught in the seminary.

[21] Ayatollah Shaykh Ali Al-Shaykh Baqir Al-Jawahiri (d. 1340 AH) was a Marja in the Holy City of Najaf. He was a distinguished teacher, poet, and a man of letters.

Experts Meeting to Select the A'lam

> *Would you prefer that a significant number of experts — like the students of bahth kharij[22] in the seminary that are recognized for their virtue and piety — deliberate every time that a Marja passes so that they may advise people on who they see is best fit for people to follow?*

This proposal would only complicate things further if it is implemented, because it cannot be applied properly.

I note the following concerns:

1) The "significant" number here is essentially arbitrary;
2) Students who have attended *bahth kharij* vary in how long they have studied;
3) There is also a range of the professors teaching, which has a direct correlation to the students that would be considered to be experts to give testimony in this matter. The qualification of the professor has an impact on the qualification of the student;
4) The students themselves have varying degrees of intellectual and scientific capability and aptitude;
5) The testimony given in regards to a student's virtue and piety is not rigorously implemented with regards to the number of testimonies as well as the scientific

---

[22] Bahth Kharij – or advanced seminars – refers to the highest level of seminary studies. – Eds.

and religious qualifications needed for the witnesses and is the standard for accepting their testimony; and

6) Moreover, those deliberating in this matter can very well differ amongst themselves – and the issue would remain unresolved.

These brief points that we mentioned are not to be argumentative or stubborn; rather, the most basic observation of civil election laws can attest that this proposal is not a good idea to resolve or organize these matters. It would only open more doors to disagreement and division. Affairs much less significant than this topic have seen problems and further discord, requiring appeal to courts of proper jurisdiction to solve the dilemma.

Moreover, this issue revolves around pinpointing what is the valid religious position. If this proposal is meant to be binding, it would need religious evidence and satisfactory proof that is sufficiently convincing to employ such a proposal. If it is meant to end the disagreement that exists in this matter, then the proof to argue for this method must be unequivocally clear and accepted by all. It is implausible that anyone can come up with such proofs.

If the result offered by this proposal is not binding, then disagreement will continue. Just as responses can be made to the many individual testimonies with opposing statements and those testifying can be questioned and discredited – the same can occur with the group testimony that this proposal would adopt.

Moreover, if the intent here is to scrutinize this subject and restrict it in a particular way that would prohibit diversity in opinion and streamline a uniform view such that any opposing view would lose religious legitimacy, that intent would be advocating for institutionalizing Marjaeya which is discussed elsewhere in this book.

The concept of transforming the Marjaeya into a formal institution, with a council that appoints the next religious authority, is one we have discussed in detail and we have highlighted its shortcomings. This proposal falls short in solving the alleged setbacks of the traditional Marjaeya.

With regards to the claims of those who are unqualified, being pragmatic dictates that they will exist regardless. Restructuring the path towards reaching the position of Marjaeya only adds to the problems that exist. Lessons can be taken from the religious institutions around the world, when comparing their goals and accomplishments at their outset to what exists as of late.

The best and most important way to lessen the negative impact of unqualified claims and deviation of all types, is through sincerity and pragmatism in protecting the religious standards. This is something we consistently emphasize and is a distinct characteristic of the Religious Authority of the Shia – all due to the blessings and support of God Almighty, as well as the care of the Imam of the Time (a) who people benefit from during his occultation like the sun behind the clouds.

PLURALITY

ON THE PRESENCE OF MULTIPLE MARAJE

> *On the subject of the presence of multiple Maraje, do you consider it to be a natural thing? What is your advice to your followers in this regard?*

There is no doubt that plurality of the Maraje is a natural situation, given the fact that satisfying the qualifications of being a Marja and being the most knowledgeable are matters subject to assessment and investigation, and can thus be points of contention and disagreement. In addition, each individual has the choice to select who they wish to follow, after they have made their best efforts to ascertain who is the most knowledgeable to no avail and are otherwise unable to practice precaution.

There are also some positive aspects of having a plurality of jurists during the time of occultation, at times. If there was only one jurist he may be inclined to proceed according to his convictions without deliberation or verification, leading to undesired consequences.

In addition, such a situation may establish an aura of sanctity and holiness for him as the only individual assuming the position. That would lead to setting precedents and traditions that could then be impossible to leave, and becomes an obstacle for objective review, and will be immune from criticism or modification. Moreover, this sort of sanctity given to one individual could seriously impede the process of *ijtihad* after him.

Of course, there is no doubt that the plurality of Maraje that are followed has negative implications as well which should not be overlooked. However, these negative implications are only a natural result of not having an immaculate source for us to go back to, due to the occultation of our Imam (a). This in itself is a cause for our grief and heartbreak over his absence. It must drive us to long for the relief that comes with his return. It reminds us of our opposition towards the oppressors that caused his disappearance and robbed the world from the blessings of his presence and his direct governance over the affairs of the world.

Nonetheless, even with its perceived negative implications, this Marjaeya remains the best option after the absence of the ideal and immaculate source – the Imam (a) himself.

Our advice to our followers is that the plurality of Maraje must not be a cause for sedition, nor a reason for disunity, hatred, or accusations. They must be respectful towards others, so long as they have fulfilled their religious obligations which have been established with proof in their perspectives. They must respect all others, stand in solidarity with one another, and work with each other for the purpose of truth and in service of principle. If others choose to follow other jurists for the wrong reasons, one should restrain himself to giving them brotherly advice with calmness and wisdom – removed from any sort of condemnation, tension, or any sort of violence. That would only worsen the situation further and be a reason for more problems and sedition.

In addition to this, one must revere all of the pious scholars who act according to their preaching; one must protect their rights, honor them. May God reward them plentifully for their endeavors and efforts, remedy their shortcomings, allow us to benefit from them, and allow us – by His grace – to be of them.

GUIDING THE PEOPLE TO THE NEW MARJA

> *Do you prefer that the current Marja advises the people to follow whom he sees as most fit after him to assume the role of the Marjaeya? Just as Shaykh Sahib Al-Jawahir did, as he came closer to his end, in naming Shaykh Murtadha Al-Ansari to lead as Marja after him?*

If what is meant here is to establish a mandatory precedent or tradition to be followed, then there's no room in our system for that for the following reasons:

Firstly, there is no religious proof to commend this sort of precedent, let alone mandating it. Likewise, there is no proof to suggest that this is authoritative to such a degree that it cannot be opposed by contrary testimony from other experts. Indeed, the Marja is only one individual from amongst a pool of experts in the field. The respected sanctity of the Marja is not enough to be unequivocal in testimony in this regard. Of course, it may have an impact on people's conviction and in feeling content with that choice over the others. However, the proof would then be the conviction obtained in following that jurist after the current Marja, not the testimony of the latter.

Secondly, pinpointing the one Marja who would have the right to appoint the next Marja would be quite problematic. The Marjaeya is often shared between more than one individual in varying ways that are not institutionalized. Similarly, the proposed precedent of naming the next Marja in such a reality would open more doors for division and disagreement.

Thirdly, the Marja is not infallible. He is a human being that is tested with outside influences which may lead to being mistaken. If the appointment of the Marja is mandatory, the Marjaeya will gradually regress, as the first mistake in an appointment may result in the choice of a weak jurist that is not qualified to lead. That jurist would then be more prone to make mistakes in general, and in choosing his own successor in particular. That will trickle down generation after generation, until the Marjaeya is weakened completely with the possibility of nothing remaining at all.

Moreover, those powers of evil that are operating in the field will perceive the existence of a mandatory system in the Marjaeya and will attempt to infiltrate the system of Marjaeya, in order to influence it and to move it away from its current correct path.

For that reason, the Imams (a) told their followers to go back to the scholars, generally, without nominating any particular persons by name, with the exception of those who transmitted their teachings, such as the four emissaries of Imam Al-Mahdi (a) during the minor occultation.

This issue relates to the discussion on institutional Marjaeya, which we discuss in the next chapter.

Of course, some Maraje may advise their followers to follow a particular jurist after them because they have confidence in his ability and knowledge, like in the case of Shaykh Sahib Al-Jawahir[1] and Shaykh Murtadha Al-Ansari[2] as mentioned above. However, such nomination is not mandatory to abide

---

[1] Shaykh Muhammad Hassan Al-Shaykh Baqir, known as Sahib Al-Jawahir (1202 – 1266 AH) lived and died in the Holy City of Najaf. He was a Marja of his time, and of the great jurists of his era. One of his most notable works was *Jawahir Al-Kalam fi Sharh Sharayi' Al-Islam*.

[2] Shaykh Murtadha Al-Shaykh Muhammad Amin (1214 – 1281 AH) is a descendant of the companion of the Holy Prophet Jabir ibn Abdillah Al-Ansari. He is regarded as an innovator in the Usool school of jurisprudence in the university of the Holy City of Najaf. One of his most notable works was *Al-Makasib*.

by or uphold. For that reason, many did not necessarily oblige themselves with the Shaykh's nomination. There were a group of Maraje contemporaneous to Shaykh Al-Ansari, such as Shaykh Mahdi Kashif Al-Ghita',[3] Shaykh Muhsen Khanfar,[4] Shaykh Mashkour Al-Hawlawi,[5] and others. Sahib Al-Jawahir's nomination of Shaykh Al-Ansari did not prevent the others from becoming Maraje, nor did it prevent people from following them.

We do not support this precedent to be repeated successively, even if it is not non-mandatory. This is because such matters may be confused by the general public and they could mistake such a gesture to be one that is mandatory. Such things can be exploited and the religious law could inadvertently be corrupted.

For this reason, we do not favor the continuation of some personal approaches of solving issues by some of the honorable Maraje, as it is possible that the great respect and veneration that they hold amongst the public may lead to confusions amongst them and they might take this advice to be a religious mandatory ruling.

---

[3] Shaykh Mahdi Al-Shaykh Ali Kashif Al-Ghataa' (1226 – 1289 AH) was one of the Maraje of his time and was regarded as a unique teacher in jurisprudence and principles of jurisprudence. He was also known as a glorified poet and man of letters.

[4] Shaykh Muhsen Al-Shaykh Muhammad Khanfar (1176 – 1270 AH) was one of the Maraje of his time. He also specialized in teaching Greek medicine, mathematics, and well regarded for his wisdom and poetry.

[5] Shaykh Mashkour Muhammad Al-Hawlawi (1209 – 1271 AH) was an esteemed followed jurist. One of his most notable works was *Manasik Al-Hajj*.

TAB'EED IN TAQLID NOT PERMISSIBLE

We notice that some of the believers follow a jurist –
other than the one he follows in taqleed – in some
matters, due to the ease that is provided by the alter-
native jurist. Is this permissible?

This is not permissible. If the original Marja that the person is following is seen as the most knowledgeable and fulfills the condition of *'adala*, then he clearly has priority, and the other is no longer an authority in the scenario. How can it then be permissible to move from the one whose authority has been established to one whose authority is not established?

If both are equal and none have prevalence in this respect, then – as mentioned previously – the initial principle is that an individual should take the most precautious position amongst the edicts of the two mujtahids. However, since that is extremely difficult and God is merciful, then what we are certain of is the permissibility of choosing to follow one of the two mujtahids in all their edicts.

As for choosing at will – choosing the edict that is more agreeable, or that which is more close to one's desires and personal whims – then there is no certainty in this being per-missible. This is especially so, considering that the method mentioned earlier is the closest path to abiding to the actual laws of Islam, and is the precautious path that must be fol-lowed. Indeed, if choosing at will were allowed, and one chooses the easiest of the two edicts in every scenario, amongst the edicts of many jurists, then he will be certainly negligent in many of his duties and will fail to undertake them.

Institutional Marjaeya

Establishing an Institution to Select the Marja'?

> *In some circles, the idea of establishing an institution*
> *to select the Marja' has been suggested, whereby a*
> *council of scholars would be organized and tasked*
> *with appointing the leading jurist. What is your view*
> *of this idea?*

Our view of this idea is similar to our view of the idea of appointing a caliph over the Muslims by the people – which was an idea adopted by those who opposed the path of the Holy Household (a).

Regardless, that idea imposed itself onto the people and they accepted and submitted to its new reality. Power controlled the interpretation and setting the framework for this idea, so much so that it became without any substantive meaning or boundaries. It became another slogan for the caliph's accession to power through force, using the name of the people. Time passed and the idea dissolved, as power no longer needed the caliphate and instead sufficed itself with mere dominion.

The Marjaeya, because of its religious nature, is grounded in the purpose of relieving one's burden of obligation before God. It is our vindication for the choices we will be called on and judged for on the Day of Judgment. Thus, it must be based on the sufficient religious evidence that can stand as proof before God on that great day.

The free and independent Marjaeya – based on the freedom of each individual to choose his Marja to follow and whom he is content with in fulfilling his religious duties – has been one which the Shia have adhered to over the long centuries from the time of the Imams (a) until today. Its validity in the eyes of the Sharia with sufficient proofs and evidence has been established. It is this system which our scholars have worked hard to build, even with the many differences amongst them on the particularities.

The general public should be cautious for their own sake in regards to the subject of following a jurist, just as they take care in all other matters of religion, such as the *'adala* of the leader of a congregational prayers and that of the witness giving testimony, the ritual purity of water used for ablution, the lawfulness of the clothes one prays in, and the money used in transactions – due care must be practiced. "God does not task any soul beyond its capacity."[1]

This idea of institutionalized Marjaeya, whereby it is assumed that religious legitimacy would only be given to a jurist who the institution chooses, cannot be adopted from a religious standpoint except by provision of sufficient religious proof for it and for all its principles and fundamentals, such as the issue of who has the right to be a part of this council, and the extent of its power in regards to the appointment of the Marja only, or also to supervise him or depose him if he no longer qualifies.

How many members will this council be comprised of? What are the necessary qualifications of knowledge and piety to be on this council, and how would that be ascertained from amongst them? If they are to disagree amongst themselves, what would be the outcome? These are just a few questions and issues in this regard.

Furthermore, if the task of this mentioned institution is to remove any sort of conflict in the matter of Marjaeya then it must necessarily have indisputable proof for its case.

We do not think anyone would have such evidence, especially given that the Shia have been deducing their jurisprudence the way they have for over a thousand years now after the occultation of the Imam (a) and have yet to produce such proof.

---

[1] The Holy Quran, 2:286.

Is it possible that the Imam (a) would leave his Shia anticipating the lengthy duration of absence – as it has been shown in the texts[2] – without it becoming clear what sort of system of Marjaeya they would have to solve the religious dilemmas they face daily? That we should wait over a thousand years for the Marjaeya that would be suggested, not knowing by whom and how?

These points are all merely from the religious standpoint. Regarding noting the positives and negatives, we do not deny that there are negatives that exist when it comes to the current state of non-institutional Marjaeya. The negative aspects arise from a number of factors, amongst them being the lack of restrictions on those who wish to claim the position of Marja, the existence of multiple Maraje, the differences in perspectives, and, many times, the succeeding Marja not fully utilizing the capacities and means built by previous Maraje.

All of these challenges, however, should not stir people up to push toward change without weighing each of the two options, comparing their positives and negatives, reflecting on what is the best option and the most practically feasible. It is important to keep in mind how often people's emotions and reactive inclinations end in unfathomable consequences.

The Marjaeya as it currently exists, with all the downsides that may exist, has proven to be formidable in leading the Shia for this long period of time – for over a thousand years. It has given its people a sense of completeness, elevated their status,

---

[2] Al-Sadouq, *Kamal Al-Deen*, 378.

clarified their stance, preserved its truths, safeguarded their values, and retained their autonomy. The Marjaeya was able to do this all without coalescing to any global powers. It did not submit before them, nor was it silent.

It is remarkable that the religion of Islam – which God willed to be eternal and everlasting so as to be the guide for humanity – faced a perilous and foretold schism after the passing of the Holy Prophet (s). Domination went to those who took political authority and claimed to be the representative and spokesman of Islam through evangelization, conquest, and plunder.

Shia Islam – for which the Messenger of God (s) planted the seed from the beginning of his message, and established its foundations and brought it to its completion towards the end of his life, which God perfected and clarified – was, after the Holy Prophet's (s) last breaths, was adhered to by barely a few individuals who held on to this message. These individuals were not able to speak in the name of Shia Islam because it was not yet fully recognized as a reality.

After some time, Shiism was again able to breathe and begin its quiet movement, by the grace of God and the patience and wisdom of the Imams (a). This movement was reinforced with the solidarity of the Shia and the many sacrifices they had to make along the way. As such, they were able to impose themselves as a reality and Shia Islam came to be recognized gradually.

Others would engage with Shias based upon this recognition, reaching the point of today where Shia Islam is acknowledged on a global level. Shiism truly represents Islam and is the real embodiment of its message. Although Shia Islam has been attacked by various powers, it has remained resilient and formidable.

Despite all of this, it does not have an apparent leader, after the occultation of its immaculate leadership (a), except the independent Marjaeya which is supported only by God and the Imam of the Time (a). It benefits from the Imam even during his occultation, just as one benefits from the sun when the clouds cover it.[3]

We can come to understand the importance of this leadership, which has persevered through about eleven centuries, if we are to compare the state of Shiism at its onset to the state of Shiism as it is today. We can see Shiism's clarity and purity after this long period of struggle, and the great gains and accomplishments it has achieved. This concept can be further understood and will become clearer when we compare it to other Muslim schools of thought. How did they begin and where are they now?

What is truly both intriguing and enlightening about the Marjaeya is the fact that Shiism, which was deprived of power for long centuries, was given an empire in Iran a few centuries ago; the Marjaeya sent its blessings and worked with it for a period of time, but it never dissolved or fused itself into the

---

[3] Al-Majlisi, *Bihar Al-Anwar*, 32:250.

body of the state. It did not merge with the government or regime just as so many other religious institutions did when their sect assumed power in their countries.

Rather, the Marjaeya kept its integrity as a spiritual overseer, holding strong to its values and principles. It would try to influence the direction of the state when it saw a path for it. If the state did not respond affirmatively, the Marjaeya would in turn reject the state's positions and deal with their own government as it would deal with other states. Such principled positions would indeed cause the Marjaeya and the associated seminaries difficulties and hardships, and suffered tragedies. All of this was due to the genuine character of the Marjaeya and its solidarity in fulfilling its role and obligation. Because of the nature of its organization, it is not restricted by any particular structure or institution. Accordingly, it cannot be seized and controlled nor can it be absorbed into the orbit of a state or government.

The fruit of this is vivid in comparing Mustapha Kamal Ataturk in Turkey and Rida Pahlavi in Iran. They came at the same time, with the decline of western colonialism in the Middle East. They both had similar designs – to overcome what had remained of each nation's Islamic thought and presence. Ataturk went a step further than Pahlavi. He eliminated the caliphate that had been so revered and officially announced the establishment of a secular state. Furthermore, he separated the Turks from their cultural heritage on some of the most fundamental levels, including replacing their Arabic alphabet with the Latin alphabet.

He was successful in his designs and its results can still be seen today. To this day his popularity in Turkey is one to be reckoned with.

Rida Pahlavi, on the other hand, failed miserably in his plans. The Iranian people were outraged during the period of Pahlavi's regime, and continue to curse him after his departure. This is even though he ruled for a considerably longer time and his policies were less inhibitive of religion.

There are many enlightening examples that can be found in more detailed accounts of history regarding the Marjaeya and its leadership over the years. They cannot all be recounted here, but a fair-minded researcher will find them easy to come by.

With regards to the Marjaeya by institution – meaning that the legitimacy of the Marja is dictated by the choice of this institution – it has not gone through a real test of experience until now.

It will never be able to go through this experience after what we discussed previously from a religious legal point of view. It will remain an idea and a hope – whether suggested with good intentions or not – against the traditional sense of the individual Marjaeya and its downsides. These supposed negativities associated with the Marjaeya have been blown out of proportion with the hopes of inflaming feelings against the Marjaeya, all the while neglecting – intentionally or not – the real negativities that come with the idea of institutional Marjayea.

The most significant downside to the institution would be it becoming an easy target for infiltration as a central specialized organization. Those wishing to infiltrate the school of thought and its leadership will work in an organized fashion using deception, bribery, lies, and intimidation – things that people of principle will not use and cannot compete with in turn.

If others do infiltrate the institution it will be easy for them to take control of it and see the results they want by their crooked aforementioned methods. Take the example of the council that resulted in Uthman's caliphate, which later resulted in the empowerment of the Umayyads over the fate of the Muslims. In such a way, infiltrators will be able to change the course of the people, abandon Islamic principles, and will not hesitate to renounce those who oppose them. The decision is theirs alone. After all, no one would have legitimacy to speak out against them since legitimacy would be for the institution alone.

From here we can infer the ease for enemies to infiltrate such an institution, either by themselves or through the use of collaborators who are deviant, ill-hearted, weak, or insatiable. When such individuals infiltrate the institution they will inevitably push it in a direction for their own selfish benefits. By that, Shiism would lose its faithful religious authority that has guided its people for over a thousand years, leading them to their current position such that it has become a burden and source of concern for the oppressors.

We can look at the religious institutions of some of the other faiths, as well as the humanitarian, governmental, and international institutions around the world. Many of them have strayed from their noble goals that they were supposedly established to achieve. Instead, some have even neglected those goals altogether and transformed into establishments of corruption and treachery, or have become subservient to such organizations or acquiesce to them.

One of the first establishments in Islam was the establishment of the Shura (the Council) whose members were from the 'foremost Muslims.' After that came Al-Tahkeem (the Arbitration), and that was followed by a number of other institutions based on the divergent schools of thought in Islam. We can see examples of institutions from other faiths, such as the Vatican. On an international level, consider the League of Nations, the United Nations Security Council, as well as the other councils and organizations that have followed. Similarly, you have the institutions established by the different parliaments of nations that have so often strayed from the noble causes they were established for. Even establishments like the Norwegian Nobel Committee – who controls it? And for whose interest does it operate? There are countless other examples.

I still remember a matter that took place during the 1980s, when the Marjaeya carried out its honorable role in resisting the spread of communism in Iraq. This drew religious individuals closer to the Marjaeya and confirmed their belief in it – even though some had been previously aggravated by the negative implications of the plurality of jurists, which they saw as an obstacle to the Marjaeya in accomplishing its goals and objectives.

It should not be veiled from the believers, may God protect them and aid them in their trials, that disagreement is a natural thing. The Imams (a) lived with their followers with direct communication between them for a period of about three centuries. They saw the disagreements that took place amongst their followers, be they well-intentioned or not, and they voiced their concerns about it, as did the Shia themselves. The Imams (a) were certainly aware of the magnitude of the occultation and the greater complexities that would follow and face the Shia. If there was a better system than the Marjaeya of the individual which is free from any institutionalization, the Imams (a) would have known it. If they would have known of it, they would not have kept that from their followers who were to face such a difficult test. Instead, they emphasized that we are to be sincere in our work, to fear God the Almighty, to be wary of seeking fame, power, and following our whims, and to have self-control and reform ourselves within.

In reality, in the absence of the direct infallible leadership, there is the inevitable possibility of mistake, be it on purpose or accident, by the leadership. The free and independent system of Marjaeya relies on two primary matters in delegating the choosing of who is to be followed as a Marja to the people in general:

Firstly, the people's oversight of the Marjaeya. If the people do not like the jurist and his mannerisms, they will deny him – even if it is amongst themselves – and go towards someone else.

Secondly, the open field of scholarship and research that allows the sincere upright jurist to rise to the occasion and assume this responsibility. Therein, truth and the people of truth have a voice and a call. It then is a proof upon the people.

Similarly, the current system prevents extreme deviation from the truth, because the presence of the truth is apparent and vocal, exposes falsehood and warns the heedless of it, and stops the followers of falsehood from drowning in it. Even if those who are deviant in their ways rallied the people around them for a period of time, the strength of truth eventually dismantles deviance and awakens people's conscience.

In this way, truth remains apparent and subsists in its call. To it the excessive returns, and the lagging catch up, and away from it the dissonant will perish.

The institutional Marjaeya model blocks the path for others, as they will not be acknowledged or accredited, even if they were truthful in their call, sincere in their work, and upright in their methods. If it were to later deviate, such a problem would be hidden from the people, as they would have no clear objective truth before them to compare it to, so they may expose the deviation. If the institution's deviation became known to the people of knowledge, they would have no avenue to bring light to the matter. If they wished to voice concern and criticize the deviation, they would be ignored because they would be seen to be without legitimacy.

After some time, true teachings will be lost. Falsehood would project itself and move in the corridors of this institution and its imposed legitimacy. Any opposing message of truth will not be apparent and the proof upon the people could not be vocal.

Perhaps this is what the late Grand Ayatollah Sayyid Abul-Hassan Al-Isfahani pointed to when he said, "Order in disorder." The following has been said in his regard,

> I wished to ask him about a saying that is often relayed on his behalf, namely the phrase 'order in disorder.' I was fortunate to be in his presence. Although where he sat was a modest place, but his great status projected before my eyes and I was overwhelmed., at his class one day and realized that even though his gathering area was very modest, his prestige was overwhelming. Nonetheless, I mustered up the courage to go up to him and ask him about this phrase in a somewhat critical manner. His face lit up with a smile and he said, 'Is it possible that I would claim a contradiction?' He continued, 'Our success [i.e. the religious establishment] in this day and age exists in the lack of order.' He then explained what he said with an example. 'If a town's infrastructure is completely connected and linked from all aspects, then a blaze in one home would mean that the fire would catch on to the rest of the homes. However, if the homes were disconnected, with no clear characteristic of orderliness, then the blazing fire on one

home would not affect the rest.' I do not further explain what
I understood from his words, just as he did not explain it.
The example alone is enough to illustrate the theory."[4]

Maybe this is the secret in the short period between Prophet
Jesus (a) and Prophet Muhammad (s), and the lengthy duration of the occultation of the Awaited Imam (a). The true
teachings of religion after Jesus (a) were lost due to Christianity's formation of institutions embodying religious authority that gave credence to no one else. The institutions deviated from their creed and the religion as a whole deviated
practically. There remained no caller to truth to uphold the
divine proof upon the people – just as Salman Al-Farsi (r)
testified when he narrated how he entered into Islam.[5] God
Almighty's wisdom and compassion dictated that He renew
His proof to mankind by sending the Seal of Prophets (s).

As for the time of the occultation, God's proof shall remain
with the endurance of the consistent call of Shiism. This is
coupled with the existence of the autonomous Marjaeya that
protects the faith, speaks on its behalf, and calls the people
to it. This faith is protected by God and the Imam of the
Time (a). Through its truth, falsehood and deviation may be
exposed.

Say, 'To God belongs the conclusive argument. Had He
wished, He would have surely guided you all.'[6] *God does not*

---

[4] Majjalet Al-Daleel, year 1, issue 3.4. Safar 1344 AH. January 1947. Special
[5] Al-Majlisi, *Bihar Al-Anwar*, 22:355.
[6] The Holy Quran, 6:149.

lead any people astray after He has guided them until He has made clear to them what they should beware of.[7]

By our assessment, the call for institutional Marjaeya is not a practical proposal given that it lacks the unequivocal religious evidence to support it. It has no effect other than disrupting the traditional system of autonomous Marjaeya, which alone has religious legitimacy. The call to institutionalizing Marjaeya simply takes advantage of people's frustrations, exaggerates certain negativities out of proportion to distract people from their religious obligations, and busies them with an idea that is alluring on the surface, and causes them to neglect looking into the issues and realizing their dangers. People's good intentions are taken advantage of and their desire for reform is exploited.

For those that have called for institutionalizing Marjaeya due to its purported current negativities, with good intentions, it would have been better to call for pragmatism and sincerity, for the strengthening of the religiosity of the Marja and those who work with him. In addition, the utmost care should be taken in following religious guidelines when calling onto the believers to following a certain jurist, as well as in the believers' answers to these calls. This is so for a number of reasons.

Firstly, this is extremely significant in upholding our religious duty and relieving our burden before God. We emphasized this point in the introduction to our *Risala Amaliyya*, as well

---

[7] The Holy Quran, 9:115.

as in our message directed at the students of the seminary and the preachers. Thus, we will not reiterate those points here.

Secondly, this is one of the most crucial causes for the abundant divine blessings upon the Marjaeya. God is always with His believing servant, so long as he is with Him. God says, "As for those who strive in Us, We shall surely guide them in Our ways, and God is indeed with the virtuous."[8]

Thirdly, pragmatism and sincerity have the greatest effect on lessening the negative effects of a plurality of religious authorities.

There are some enlightening anecdotes of the Marjaeya of the past and present that show us the significance of sincerity and pragmatism. The harmony amongst the multiple Maraje was strongest in the thirteenth century after Hijra, during the era of the late Shaykh Kashif Al-Ghita and his brothers.

It is also widely known that the late Shaykh Sahib Al-Jawahir advised that people follow the late Shaykh Al-Ansari after him. He had great trust in Shaykh Al-Ansari, even though the Shaykh did not belong to his group nor was he follower of his own particular school of thought within the seminary.

The late Sayyid Al-Shirazi[9] constantly showed how much he cared about his contemporary colleague the late Shaykh Muhammad Hassan Aal Yaseen. It is said that a group of merchants from Baghdad went to Samarra carrying with them

---

[8] The Holy Quran, 29:69.
[9] Also known as: Sayyid Al-Shirazi Al-Kabeer and Al-Mujaddid Al-Shirazi

religious dues. He reprimanded them and said, "If the religious dues of the people of Baghdad are brought to us, Shaykh Muhammad Hassan Aal Yaseen and those with him will die of hunger!" When news came to Samarra that Shaykh Aal Yaseen passed away, the late Shaykh Muhammad Hirzeddine said, "I was told by a trustworthy source that Mirza Sayyid Muhammad Hussain Al-Shirazi cried for his loss. He held a memorial service in his honor in Samarra and we attended it."[10]

When Sayyid Al-Shirazi was attacked in Samarra and his son was killed during a meaningless act of sectarian violence, the jurists and scholars of the Holy City of Najaf marched on to Samarra in support and solidarity with the late Sayyid.

During our time, we witnessed the Marjaeya of our teacher and grandfather the late Sayyid Mushin Al-Hakeem, and the honorable Shaykh Muhammad Rida Aal Yaseen. The collaboration, partnership, and cooperation between the two was truly exemplary.

To this day we still feel the deep effects of sincerity and pragmatism in creating the harmony between the religious authorities and their cooperation to avoid negativity and division. Alas, we cannot detail all of this as the topic is too expansive to be fully covered here.

We wish to conclude this discussion with the significance of the religious authority relying on people of faith and exper-

---

[10] Hirzeddine, *Ma'arif Al-Rijal*, 2:233.

tise. He should consult with them and delegate responsibilities amongst specialized committees dedicated to fulfilling different duties. The responsibility is greater and more complex than to be assumed by one person alone, especially in the contemporary age with all of its added complexities. Similarly, he must support and guide the personnel of the different Islamic organizations, centers, and projects pursuing this work.

We ask God the Almighty to support those who are sincere in their work and to allow benefit to come from them. He is the guardian of the believers. God is sufficient for us, and He is the best protector.

THE MARJA AND HIS CLOSE CIRCLE

THE MARJA'S RELIANCE ON HIS CLOSE CIRCLE

> *Some have asked, why does the Marja rely on his sons and those who are close to him more than anyone else?*

This observation does not exist across the board. It differs from one Marja to the next as a result of the circumstances and situation they live in. Many Maraje were not known to be as such, even if it may be due to a lack of relatives or students who they could rely on. Some were relatively more reliant on their families. Others relied more on their students.

The most important matter here is trust, sincerity, and diligence in taking care of the Marja's affairs as well as good administration. If that cannot be found in the Marja's relatives or students he must not rely on them. One of the biggest criticisms of Uthman during his caliphate was his reliance on his unqualified relatives and the placing of the affairs of the Muslims in their hands.

If those who are close are indeed qualified, then what would be the reason not to rely on them even in specified capacities if not generally?

It has been narrated that the Commander of the Faithful (a) was criticized for relying on his family members and entrusting them with authority. He replied, "Bring me someone that is better than them so that I may entrust him with authority!"[1]

If the Marja is to see that he can trust his students or those that are close to him with these responsibilities, and that they are worthy of such responsibility, then why wouldn't he? This is especially so given that these are people that have surpassed others in sacrificing their time and effort with him before he even became a Marja to be followed by the public. They lived with him and he has tested them, and has come to know them more deeply than he would know anyone else. They know his direction, thought, and outlook – upon which he has assumed the responsibility of the Marjaeya – better than anyone else. By working within that framework and sacrificing for it, they are naturally the most suited and closest. Of course, reliance cannot be based on one's sentimental connection to another, where it would be the reason why an unrelated person who is otherwise more trustworthy and qualified is not entrusted with responsibility.

---

[1] Al-Mutazili, *Sharh Nahjul Balagha*, 15:199.

When I traveled to Iran, during the lifetime of our teacher and grandfather the late Sayyid Al-Hakeem,[2] I attended a gathering with some others. One of the individuals I met there suggested to me that the late Sayyid should exclude his sons from being involved in the administration of the Marjaeya's affairs, because he was convinced of a claim that he had attributed to some of the other Maraje.

I replied, "If you see that the Sayyid raised his sons, planting in them sincerity and trustworthiness, and knew that they were qualified for such a responsibility, then what would be the justification to leave them and seek others who are not close to him and do not know him?!"

I still remember that dark night in the Holy City of Najaf, during my late grandfather's illness, when we were informed by telephone of his worsening condition. It was in the beginning of the month of Safar, about two months before he passed away. He suffered a severe heart attack, and because of it would only have weeks to live. Most of our relatives rushed to Baghdad to be at his side. No one remained in Najaf except his eldest son, my uncle, the late Ayatollah Sayyid Yousuf Al-Hakeem and some of the elders of the family. I stayed behind as well. After Maghrib prayers that night, we

---

[2] In his administration, he relied on a number of scholarly individuals like his son Ayatollah Sayyid Yousuf Al-Hakeem, Grand Ayatollah Shaykh Muhammad Taqi Al-Faqih, Al-Hujja Al-Alam Sayyid Ali Bahreluloom, Al-Hujja Al-Adib Sayyid Muhammad Jamal Al-Hashimi, Ayatollah Sayyid Muhammad Ali Al-Hakeem, Hujjat Al-Islam wal-Muslimeen Shaykh Muhieddeen Al-Maqamani, and Al-Hujja Shaykh Hussain Ma'tooq, amongst others.

came back to our general gathering place at my late grandfather's home. Silence and worry filled the room. We expected the inevitable news at any moment.

After the gathering ended, and people had left, I walked with my late uncle on his way home. As we walked we spoke about something that seemed to be weighing heavily on his shoulders, something that he felt was even more important than losing his father. "There is no escaping death," he said, "but my issue is that the Sayyid entrusted me with authority over the public's money to spend as deemed necessary. It is difficult for me to take on this responsibility."

He mentioned a number of concerns he had. I tried to reassure him but I was not successful. We arrived at his doorstep and he asked me to come inside to continue the conversation. We spoke for long, until I said, "This money will inevitably be spent. I assure you that you will get the necessary authorization from all of those who have religious authority over such funds, from Maraje and jurists." There were many of them in Najaf. Still, he insisted on abstaining from the responsibility. He even requested, adamantly, that I travel the next day to Baghdad to inform my grandfather of his wish to abstain from this responsibility.

The request made me quite uncomfortable. It would be very hard for me to face my late grandfather and deliver that kind of information to him while he was in such a state of health. That, along with other caveats I was wary of.

Nonetheless, I reluctantly gave in, considering my uncle's situation and I agreed to his request. However, God saved me from what I had feared. It worked out that he was able to ask someone else who was already in Baghdad to deliver the information. Surely, my late grandfather was informed of my uncle's reservations. Still, he insisted that my uncle fulfill the tasks he entrusted him with, because he was confident in his qualifications, judgment, piety, and prudence. My uncle submitted and fulfilled his duties, after he had taken precaution to the furthest extent possible.

I mention this story as a historical point to derive a lesson from. If one's son will treat a trust with such prudence and caution, then what would be the justification to seek someone other than him to rely on?

It is things like this that reinforce the values of the Marja and the strength of his influence over his followers to hold strong to their ethics and principles. It reinforces the people's trust in him and those around him. The Marjaeya's place in people's hearts is elevated, just as we saw the effect our late uncle Sayyid Yousuf had on the people. They grew attached to him and stressed that they wished to follow him as the next Marja and were adamant that he accept them as such. He insisted to abstain from the post in his prudence, just as he insisted on refraining from taking responsibility, but he did not find a way to do so. This was the case even though he was qualified for the Marjayea in the eyes of many of the scholars of the Holy City of Najaf during his time – the most prominent amongst them being my late grandfather. This was seen in his treatment of Sayyid Yousef, as well as definitive accounts that have reached us stating that he directed others to Sayyid Yousuf.

But Sayyid Yousuf responded to all of this by saying that it was my grandfather who warned him of the great burdens of the Marjaeya. One day, I came to my uncle and found him so deeply affected by some of the issues before him. He said to me, "Don't get yourself tangled up in these matters."

He was so cautious of his responsibilities and so prudently upright, that he would be uncomfortable to participate in some activities that had any possibility of resulting in vanity or self-regard – like leading congregational prayers. I was told that during the lifetime of my late grandfather, particularly in the middle of his tenure as Marja, my late uncle had said, "I do these things only to abide by the orders and wishes of the Sayyid. I'm not sure what my position would be after him. I would probably leave it as I wouldn't be bound for it any-more." He carried on like that, fulfilling the role to the extent that he saw was required of him. We ask God to give him the best of rewards, and to reward all for their work and good intentions – He is surely the most merciful and the guardian of the believers.

THE MARJAEYA ESTABLISHMENT SUBMITS TO THE MARJA NOT HIS ADVISORS

> *There is a suggestion that the Marjaeya establishment is more subject to the advisors of the Marja rather than the Marja himself. What are your thoughts on this?*

This is – in its generalization – an injustice and a mischaracterization of reality. There is no general rule for this matter, and it, rather, is a matter that differs from one Marja to the other. The personality, style, and resolve of the Marja is a big factor. Also, the ease of making a decision and remaining firm in decision-making plays a big role as well. This is the case with any leadership position, and is not unique to religious authorities.

There is no problem for the working body or administration of the Marja to have an impact on decision-making and the actions of the establishment as a whole. This is a natural effect of the Marja utilizing those around him as advisors and counsel, which would definitely be a positive attribute for the Marja. As for reserving decision-making for the person of the Marja alone, that would go back to the Marja's personality and style of leadership.

We have observed a number of Maraje's distinct ability to lead and have firm control over their establishment. They coupled that with pragmatism and virtuous dealing, which was admirable and worthy of respect.

Of course, when answering this and the previous question, we do not deny that there are negatives that result here – mostly unintentional but sometimes deliberate. Our hope is that the believers are realistic and pragmatic. We pray that they are wary of the senseless campaign against the Marjaeya and the seminary that has exaggerated the negativities and fabricated others.

We have looked into some of the cases of defamation against the greatest Maraje, whom the Islamic Seminary reveres. Those who have even an ounce of dignity, let alone faith, will not commit such an act. Their sole purpose and intent is to shake people's trust in the Marjaeya – a symbol of pride for our school of thought and a sign of honor for us all. This Marjaeya is our school's path to God and the embodiment of its personality and efficacy.

God is witness to what our great scholars face as a result of their commitment to their principles, steadfastness on their positions, firmness on their path, and their refusal to work with evil powers and despots or be engulfed in their orbit. We ask God Almighty to support and bless them on this path, and to reward their work and increase their rewards – surely, He is the guardian of the believers and the supporter of the oppressed. He sufficed us, and He is an excellent trustee.

Hypothetically, if trust in the Marjaeya were to be shaken, could we fathom of an alternative that is free from any negatives? Where would the believers go? How would they reach their Lord's commandments and safeguard their faith from distortion and manipulation? And if the Marjaeya – which we condition to have the highest level of righteousness – is not fit to be trusted, then what are we to do? Are we to be without a Marjaeya? Or do we work with an untrustworthy Marjaeya, and fall into the same mistakes that others have made?

It is more becoming of the believers to reflect on themselves and their faith. Their call should be one of reform that aims to support and advocate for the Marjaeya, let alone glorify and venerate it.

Nonetheless, we emphasize on pragmatism, sincerity, piety, and virtuous conduct for the Marja himself, as well as his aides and those supporting him. These traits are to be encouraged for anyone who rises to this position, as well as those working with him and joining his movement. In addition, there should be a quiet renunciation of those who neglect these traits so that their wares may be known. By this, only those who are truly qualified with these traits will take on this trust. This should all be observed with complete wariness from such people and from defamation and false rumors, where personal interests and individual sentiments take play.

The trust is truly great and the responsibility is immense. God is the overseer of this and He knows what the eyes cannot see and what the hearts conceal.

Moreover, we mentioned in a previous chapter that the Marjaeya is based on the people's oversight of the Marja. Thus, they must fulfill their duty from their place and not take it for granted like an indifferent bystander.

Let the test that we are living in be a motivator towards fulfilling our duty, safeguarding the trust and upholding our responsibility toward this noble principle. In this spirit, let us reinforce the line of the Marjaeya. God is the guardian of success, He is sufficient for us, and He is the best protector.

THE CHALLENGES OF TODAY

THE MOTIVATION BEHIND LECTURES ON ETHICS

> *It has become known about you that you give a particular emphasis on delivering lectures on ethics and civics during the holy month of Ramadan as well as other seasons. Do you see that this is a persisting necessity during our day and age?*

This is a necessity for every age and applies to every individual no matter his or her status. The Holy Prophet (s) says in one noble tradition, "Remember, join together, and discuss. Surely, discussion cleanses the hearts. For hearts rust like swords, and they are cleansed by discussion."[1]

This significant point is emphasized in the Holy Quran, the narrations from the Holy Prophet (a) and his Household (a),

---

[1] Al-Kulayni, *Al-Kafi*, 1:41.

as well as the traditions from the previous prophets and saints. It became custom to hold gatherings for this purpose of giving people advice and guidance. One of those gatherings was held in the courtyard of the Holy Shrine of Imam Ali (a), where the late Shaykh Ja'far Al-Shushtari spoke. People from all groups attended, including renowned religious authorities of the Holy City of Najaf. In addition, there are numerous private sessions and gatherings, as well as ethics courses held by the accomplished professors of the seminary.

Preferably, this is what should be considered and emphasized in this day and age. We live in a time where materialism reigns and the devil's strings have strengthened. The tones of leniency, indulgence, and justifying wrong are oft too common.

If holding special sessions for advice, guidance, and counsel on ethics and civics are not possible, then the speakers of the pulpit should give particular focus to it during the majalis[2] of Imam Hussain (a). Such gatherings, as well as any other religious or community events, should be held to shed light on ethics through the Holy Quran, the noble narrations, and the teachings and lives of the Ahlulbayt (a), as well as the lives of the closest of their pure companions. They should be sure to stay clear from indulging in self-generated and opinionated verdicts that have no basis whatsoever.

---

[2] Majalis is the plural form of majlis – literally meaning a gathering or assembly, but in Islamic contexts refers to a gathering of commemoration for Imam Hussain or another member of the Prophet's Household where their tragedies are eulogized. – Eds.

If this cannot be attained, then people must turn to the Holy Quran, the sermons of the Holy Prophet (s) and his Household (a), and their many supplications. Through their teachings and their life stories, we may cleanse our hearts and reform our souls. Their words are light, their cause is guidance, their direction is piety, their acts are virtue, their tradition is benevolence, and their character is generosity.

Praise be to God for allowing us to hold on to them, and sufficing ourselves with their rope – the rope of God. We ask Him to support us to be firm on this path.

THE ABSENCE OF THE IMAM IN THE CONSCIENCE OF THE SHIA

Imam Al-Mahdi (aj) is absent from the conscience of many of the Shia even though they believe in him. What are the ways that you see can strengthen their consciousness of his presence?

Every reality that is absent physically requires that an active effort and focus be given to it with constant reflection and contemplation, and to never be heedless to the thought of it, in order to build its presence in one's conscience. By doing this, its effect will be seen in the conduct of those who believe in it. This is something we particularly emphasize, as discussed in more depth in our treatise to the seminarians and preachers.

One of the most fundamental hidden truths is the existence of Imam Al-Mahdi (aj) and his role and effect on the order of the universe, and especially in the affairs of his followers – as well as greater humanity – in protecting their concerns and supporting their movement. We benefit from him like we benefit from the sun behind the clouds.[3] The world cannot endure without an Imam, and if he were to be taken away the world would cease to exist.[4]

It is incumbent on the believers to care for having his presence in their conscience and to focus on him from within. They are to reflect, contemplate, and connect with him through the many supplications and visitations that have been taught by him and his infallible forefathers. This connection can be strengthened by turning to the Imam (aj) during their tests and trials, for the test that he endures has been the longest in duration and the greatest in hardship. Beseech him in your endeavors and your difficulties. Call onto God through him, as God administers His affairs through the Imam's (aj) hands. Surely, the Imam (aj) is the best intercessor to God in this era.

Moreover, the believers should connect themselves to their Imam (aj) through their scholars – for they represent his path and fulfill some of his role in his absence. As the noble narration tells us, they are the proof upon his followers and he is the proof of God.[5]

---

[3] Al-Majlisi, *Bihar Al-Anwar*, 32:250.

[4] Al-Kulayni, *Al-Kafi*, 1:178-180.

[5] Al-Amili, *Wasai'l Al-Shia*, 18:101.

Even when we take a look at the prevalent corruption and oppression taking place in the world, we realize that it is a cause for our remembrance of him and our sorrow due to his occultation. We should await his reappearance and anticipate the relief that he will bring to us all, because he will fill the world with justice and equity after it is filled with oppression and tyranny.

It has been narrated from the Imams (a) that the followers should be deterred from wrongdoing because their actions are revealed to the Prophet (s) and the living Imam (aj). When they witness the sins and wrongdoings of their followers they are deeply wounded.[6]

If people were to take this all into consideration and seriously reflect on it, it would greatly better their situations. They love and revere the Prophet (s) and the Imam (aj), and thus would not accept it upon themselves to hurt them by their own wrongdoing.

We ask God to make us firm in our allegiance to his authority and our preparation for his return. We ask God to bestow upon us the kindness, benevolence, mercy, care, supplication, thoughts, and intercession of the Imam (aj); and to not deprive us of it in this life or the next.

---

6 Al-Kulayni, *Al-Kafi*, 1:219.

THE CURRENT STATE OF MISTRUST BETWEEN SOCIETY AND THE CLERGY

There seems to be a state of mistrust between some of our communities and the clergy. Could you provide some advice and direction on how to mitigate this situation?

This is by far one of the gravest and most complex problems our school of thought is tested with. Nonetheless, it is a good sign as it is befitting of the school's solidarity and perpetuity. It shows that our society does not follow the clergy blindly, and thus no one person can steer the community away from the straight path of the school of thought, if he succumbs to his desires. Nor can external pressures infiltrate the school to deviate it like other sects and communities have experienced.

When a member of the clergy knows that he is subject to criticism and scrutiny, he is indeed more alert. Accordingly, he will avoid pitfalls and situations of suspicion and accusation. He will instead be more cautious and be motivated towards integrity and refinement.

Nevertheless, all parties must be mindful not to cross the boundaries that God has established for us, and must be cautious not to do so in the name of self-liberation and out of impulsiveness. We must seek the pleasure of God and be sincere with Him.

It is incumbent on clerics and preachers to honor their duties to the fullest extent in the best of ways. They are to avoid engaging in any sort of negative situations to the best of their ability. In addition, they should be open to dialogue, listen attentively to constructive criticism and be responsive to feedback. Of course, they should not do these things for the sake of pleasing people, nor should they sacrifice their values or obligations no matter what the price.

Likewise, members of the general community need to encourage uprightness, the fulfillment of obligations, and reject deviation and perversion, whatever the cause of it may be. They should be wary of destructive criticism that is neither responsible nor fair.

Of course, there is an important part of this issue that should be discussed here, and that is the issue of monies and funds which find themselves in the hands of the clergy, some of whom have not made good use of this money. The expectation is that they expend this money on supporting the propagation of the faith and helping the poor and needy.

People have not always sensed this from the members of the clergy, however. Instead, it seems to some people that the clergy take the money for their own benefit, living in comfort through it, and spending opulently and recklessly from it. Their perceptions have dictated a negative reflection of the clergy with many people, and much of the good they do has been lost in people's eyes. Some have come to believe that members of the clergy did not become clerics to undertake their religious obligations and their duties to call people to

God, but instead did so for their own monetary gain and un-lawful earnings. These perceptions have tarnished people's trust in the clergy and has cast these suspicions of them. The situation can become more dire and the repercussions could be severe.

Thus, clerics and preachers who are sincere in their work – upon which the fruits of their efforts will come about – must do the following:

Firstly, they must distance themselves from situations of sus-picion where they can be wrongly accused. They should not ask others for money and must not position themselves in a way to receive it either. And if they are offered money, as a gift or personal assistance, they should not take it.

Moreover, if the money is in the form of religious dues they should not accept it for themselves. They are to take it to the Marja that the person paying the religious dues follows, or the Marja of the cleric's prudent choosing if the payer of the dues leaves it up to them. The cleric is to receive a receipt from the office of the Marja and deliver it to the payer of the dues, so that delivery of those dues is confirmed. Further-more, the clerics will coordinate with the Marja in regards to how to spend that money received, in ways that please God.

This does include the cleric being paid from that money for his personal needs in compensation for his services, and as a liaison between the Marja and the people. This is to ensure that the cleric is honored, supported, and not put in a posi-tion of need before people.

Our late grandfather, Sayyid Al-Hakeem, emphasized this with his closest and most trusted liaisons and representatives. He did this to ensure that they were far from positions of suspicion or accusation. Indeed, that was one of the best results of his era.

Secondly, members of the clergy should not expand their wealth and spend it on themselves. They should distance themselves from appearing to be hoarding money and indulging in extravagance and luxury. This is to be implemented even if their earnings are from their own personal earnings, let alone being in possession of religious dues.

After satisfying their needs, the clerics should spend any surplus of money on religious services projects and helping the needy. They should care for their needs, alleviate their pain and hardship, and aid them wherever possible.

In all of this, and before anything else, is the pleasure of God. That is the most important element in obtaining success and blessings in any work. Furthermore, it will lead to ensuring people's trust in the clergy, so that they may be content with them, listen to them, heed to their advice and wisdom, and work with them in serving this noble religion which has persevered its true ideals due to the strength and clarity of its proofs – as well as the efforts, sacrifices, perseverance and patience of its followers across the ages and despite calamities.

We ask God that He allow us to be of the ones who work in this pursuit. We pray that He is pleased with us and accepts us, as He is the Compassionate, the Merciful.

SPENDING RELIGIOUS DUES WITHOUT THE CONSULTATION OF THE JURIST

Some people spend the religious dues by themselves without referring to and consulting the qualified jurist. Their justification is that the way they are spending the money is within the scope of what is pleasing to God and Imam Al-Mahdi (aj). What are your thoughts on this?

It is a person's right to do that if his Marja – whom he has chosen to follow based on religious standards – does not mandate his followers to consult with the jurist in spending the religious dues. If that is not the case, such action would fall outside the scope of what God has ordered us in reverting to our jurists, let alone the Imam (aj) who possesses the ultimate rights over the religious dues. It has been narrated that the Imam (aj) said, "In regards to the contemporary matters, refer to the narrators of our tradition, for they are my proof upon you, and I am the proof of God."[7]

A believer pays his religious dues so that he can free himself from those liabilities and to be relieved of his burden before

---

[7] Al-Amili, *Wasai'l Al-Shia*, 18:101.

God. He does this for his own salvation from detriment. Yet, how can a believer achieve this if he is to transgress the boundaries set for him and the guidelines required in following a jurist – all purposed in relieving his burden of obligation before God? Why would someone be so careless in fulfilling these duties and allow himself to be outside the boundaries that the religion has established?

To take this route would inherently cause harm to the existence of Shiism and its functionality. It causes lawlessness in the system of religious dues and rights. If people continue to act based on individual and personal inclinations, as well as indulging themselves in emotion rather than reason, it will gradually create a deviation and distancing from religion.

Of course, if the person paying the religious dues is experienced in worthy causes for the religious dues and has the ability to ensure proper funding for them, or he has his own views on how funds should be spent, it is possible for him to discuss his opinions with the jurist and coordinate with him. His perspective will be heard, especially on the basis of my edict, which states that the responsibility over the religious dues is shared between the jurist and the individual paying them.

This would be a source of strength for the Marjaeya and unity for the Shia, as well as a solution for many problems and prevention for many expected negative repercussions. As God says, "Cooperate in piety and Godwariness, but do not cooperate in sin and aggression, and be fearful of God. Indeed God is severe in retribution."[8]

We have a more elaborate discussion on this issue, directed to the students of the seminary and the preachers, that would be worth referring to.[9]

THE MARJAEYA AND MODERN MEANS OF COMMUNICATION

> *What is your view on the Marjaeya's openness to modern means of communication, such as the internet and satellite channels, and what is required in that regard of resources and administration?*

The Marjaeya is in dire need of such modern means of communication to expand the scope of the work and the benefit it provides to people. This is especially needed given the fact that the believers are spread across the world, and such technology allows for greater and more beneficial services

The Marjaeya, and the rest of the religious functions, have always been open to modern technology and means of communication, without hesitation. From the printing press and electricity to television and the telegraph, the Marjaeya utilized these means from their outset in spreading the message

---

[8] The Holy Quran, 5:2.
[9] Al-Hakeem, *Risala Abawiya*, 48.

of the faith to the world. Through these mediums its voice was heard, its message was delivered, and its proof was established.

We are supportive of any new technology that is beneficial and does not contradict the teachings of our faith or harm our values, ethics, and honor.[10] God said, "And say, 'Go on working: God will see your conduct, and His Apostle and the faithful [as well]…'"[11] And in the Holy Quran God is described, "It is He who created for you all that is in the earth."[12]

It is true that the Marjaeya may not hurry to adopt some of these new means of communication. This is often due to a lack of financial or human resources. It may also be a temporary precautionary measure, due to possible negativities in the utilization of such means, such that harm is feared, or that the harm outweighs the benefits, or due to it being viewed to be of a bad reputation which contradicts the sacred position that the Marjaeya holds. This of course cannot be compromised for the great weight and responsibility the Marjaeya assumes.

All in all, the outcome may differ depending on the available resources, the current circumstances, and the varying per-

---

[10] The official website for the office of H.E. Grand Ayatollah Sayyid Al-Hakeem can be visited at: www.alhakeem.com.

[11] The Holy Quran, 9:105.

[12] The Holy Quran, 2:29.

spectives on a secondary level. This does not impact that fundamental or primary favorable view, held by our faith, on modern means of communication.

THE STRENGTH OF THE SHIA

ELEMENTS OF STRENGTH FOR THE SHIA SCHOOL OF THOUGHT

What are the elements of strength for the Shia school of thought, and the movement of their followers, that allowed them to withstand the many trials and hardships endured over such a long span of time?

The elements for the strength of the Shia school, its movement and followers, are numerous. These strengths have allowed the school and its followers to withstand the trials of history and hardships that have shaped the school for more than a thousand years.

The first strength of the school of thought is its own intrinsic strength, derived from the fact that it is the school of truth and excellence, of strong proof and dazzling evidence – in any intellectual, logical and fair discourse – and it is free from contradictions, inconsistencies, and discrepancies. This school of thought has the ideal solution to the issue of succession to the Holy Prophet (s), which is the fundamental schism in Islam, by which this school of thought has distinguished itself.

Secondly, the holy Imams (a) hold a distinct position in the hearts of Muslims by virtue of their relationship to the Holy Prophet (s), as well as the tremendously many virtues and merits they hold, which have been narrated from the Prophet (s) and which their own noble existences speak of, whereby their great knowledge, their holiness and their monumental personalities have become undeniable. They imposed themselves upon friend and foe, and they became the insignia of pride for their followers and adorers.

Additionally, the Imams (a) stood out in their wisdom in leading and educating the Shia. They strengthened their allegiance to the Prophet (s) and his Household (a), through their sacred teachings, supplications, and psalms. The way the Imams (a) raised their followers was unique in two primary matters:

1) Through mastering the disciplines of intellect and reason, as well as logical deduction and the power of proofs and evidence; and

2) Implementing superb ethics in interaction and integration, and displaying great morality and gentleness to others. This is especially evident when comparing them to others, as will be discussed further in the

coming discussion on Ibn Abi Al-Hadid and his book *Sharh Nahjul Balagha.*

Thirdly, the trials and hardship that befell the Holy House-hold (a) is an element of strength. It caused the following results:

1) People gravitated toward them, because people are innately inclined to favor and support the oppressed.

2) Their followers were able to endure hardship and be patient throughout by following their example.

3) The introduction of religious events and seasons that brought the Shia closer to their Imams (a) and their principles, especially with the pilgrimage to their shrines, the commemorations of their tragedies, and adherence to their slogans, etc.

At the same time, this is the strongest propagation for the honorable school of thought and bringing people closer to it, as the Shia movement has always been true to this.

Fourthly, the Marjaeya and the Islamic seminary have always been independent, both financially and methodically, whereby their leadership could not have been compromised. What allowed for this is the presence of scholars of high standing in knowledge and faith, firm on the principles, protecting the teachings of the school from distortion and corruption. In addition to the scholars was the presence of numerous believers who made it their priority to find the truth through those scholars. The persistence of the scholars became a factor in distinguishing them as a living sacred body of spiritual leadership that is highly respected and very active.

Fifthly, the school of thought was distinguished by the continuance of the divine touch through the miracles of the Imams (a). These miraculous events occurred in appropriate times in an undeniably unstaged manner, similar to electric shocks to people's conscience. They rejuvenated people's connection to the school of thought and its symbols, and they manifested their rights and their reality, and their connection to God, as well as His support for them.

Sixthly, the failure of other groups – Islamic or otherwise – in appeasing people and trying to gain their support also was a point of strength for the Shia. In the end those groups spread only through force and oppression. The Shia benefited, whether they wished for it or not, from this point of weakness that other groups had – whereby their crimes were denounced, their ideas were debunked, and they were shown to be an utter failure.

By this, the Shia school of thought gained the love and support of the oppressed, as well as the opposition of the oppressors. Tyrants and oppressors swore vengeance against this school of thought, especially after failing to succeed against the Shia theologically. The resolve of the Shia in their creed, against all odds, strengthened their morale and their voice. Being oppressed, standing against oppression, and sacrifice, became medals of honor for them.

Perhaps this is what is referred to in the narrations from our Imams (a) that God has aided us against our enemies by giving them foolishness. They chose to ignore the fact that true belief does not crumble before financial pressures, oppression, or subjugation. Instead, belief will only become more deeply rooted and grow in solidarity and strength.

The seventh and final point is perhaps the most important element of strength for the Shia. The call of Shiism is the Word of God – the only one in this world that battles the waves of sedition, deviation, blasphemy, hypocrisy, disintegration, decadence, oppression and subjugation.

Thus, Shiism is guided by God, safeguarded with His support, and protected by His care, so that His proof may be complete upon the people. "…So that he who perishes might perish by a manifest proof, and he who lives may live on by a manifest proof…"[1]

This is the blessing of God upon the believers; they must honor the right of this blessing, be thankful for it, and know how to safeguard and care for it. Indeed, it is by gratefulness and thanks that blessings last. God says "If you are grateful, I will surely enhance you [in blessing], but if you are ungrateful, My punishment is indeed severe."[2]

Finally, "Those who disobey his orders should beware lest an affliction should visit them or a painful punishment should

---

[1] The Holy Quran, 8:42.
[2] The Holy Quran, 14:7.

befall them."[3] We seek God's protection from such disobedience which will lead to Him abandoning us, and from deviation, and ill outcomes.

RUMORS MADE AGAINST THE SHIA AND STANDING AGAINST THEM

> *There are a number of rumors and slander campaigns made against the Shia from different groups. How should the Shia counter this, both in thought and behavior?*

This intense campaign is something natural and expected, given the Shia's unique position in standing for truth, and their alignment against the worldwide tendency towards being dominated by materialism and immorality. The Shia have not bowed to this temptation nor do they work with it; instead they choose to expose it by their own righteous conduct and by rejecting crime and injustice. Therefore, the Shia must acclimatize themselves to these sorts of campaigns against them and prepare themselves for it. This is not foreign to our history as a school of thought, as even worse campaigns have been waged against the Shia for quite a long time.

Our hope is in God, and the blessing of Imam Al-Mahdi (aj), to support and aid the Shia until they emerge victorious and

---

[3] The Holy Quran, 24:63.

rise above the fray. God says, "So be patient. Indeed the out-come will be in favor of the Godwary."[4] He also said,

> *Have you not regarded how God has drawn a parable? A good word is like a good tree: its roots are steady and its branches are in the sky. It gives its fruit every season by the leave of its Lord. God draws these parables for mankind so that they may take admonition. And the parable of a bad word is that of a bad tree: uprooted from the ground, it has no stability. God fortifies those who have faith with a constant creed in the life of this world and in the Hereafter, and God leads astray the wrongdoers, and God does whatever He wishes.*[5]

In facing this negative campaign, we must take several steps.

Firstly, we need to avoid violence in all shapes and forms. Violence is a display of weakness which harms the person himself; rather, one's enemies can exploit, exaggerate, and use it against you, leading to undesirable complications. Further-more, reacting violently can be in itself a violation of God's law – which we have to protect and follow in all of our affairs, especially in matters pertaining to our belief and principles.

We must practice patience and forbearance. We must present ourselves and our ideas in a civil manner. Our excellence is in our character and our ethics. This was the etiquette of our Imams (a) and their followers.

---

[4] The Holy Quran, 11:49.
[5] The Holy Quran, 14:24-27.

In his biography of the Commander of the Faithful (a), Ibn Abi Al-Hadid says,

> *And as for excellence in ethics, an illuminating aura, a beautiful demeanor, and an unwavering smile, he was the one who set the example. It was so much so that his enemies would attempt to deride him even in these characteristics. These traits remained and were inherited by his followers and admirers to this very day, just as dryness, harshness, and callousness remains with the others. Those who have the most basic knowledge of people's ethics and their manners know this.*[6]

Secondly, we must have confidence in ourselves for the mere fact that we are with truth. Just as the Commander of the Faithful (a) said, "My strength does not grow by the abundance of people around me, nor does my solitude increase by their departure."[7]

It is enough for our morale that we have the awareness that we are Muslims. God says, "Should anyone follow a religion other than Islam, it shall never be accepted from him, and he will be among the losers in the Hereafter."[8] Furthermore, we are the one saved group from amongst seventy-three factions, as mentioned in the famous narration of the Prophet (s).[9] We have attached ourselves to the Prophet's Household

---

[6] Al-Mutazili, *Sharh Nahjul Balagha*, 1:25.

[7] Al-Mutazili, *Sharh Nahjul Balagha*, 16:148.

[8] The Holy Quran, 3:85.

[9] Al-Sadouq, *Al-Khissal*, 585; Al-Qayrawani, *Al-'Umda*, 74.

(a), and they are the peak of honor, faith, and sanctity by the consensus of all Muslims.

There is more that has been relayed in narrations in praise of the Shia, especially during the time of the occultation. The Shia are praised as being the true friends of God. The denizens of the Heavens look at the Shia just as we gaze upon the stars in the sky. Imam Al-Sadiq (a) said, "I am apprehensive of the many times I have narrated this to you: there is nothing between you and that you receive joy except the passing of your soul through here." And he pointed his hand towards his throat."[10] Similar narrations are too numerous to recount.

It is just as God the Almighty emphasized in His Holy Book, that the thankful ones of His servants are the very few, as are the saved amongst them. He says, "A multitude from the former [generations] and a multitude from the latter [ones]."[11] There are numerous narrations of the Prophet (s) and his Household (a) speaking to this reality as well.

Moreover, God emphasizes that the believers are tested with tribulation and calamity. He says,

> *Do you suppose that you will enter paradise though there has not yet come to you the like of [what befell] those who went before you? Stress and distress befell them and they were convulsed until the apostle and the faithful who were with him*

---

[10] Al-Barqi, *Al-Mahasin*, 175.
[11] The Holy Quran, 56:39-40.

said, 'When will God's help [come]?' Behold! God's help is indeed near![12]

Abundant narrations elaborate on this as well, especially with the context of the age of occultation which is a period of tests and trials for the Shia.

Furthermore, the narrations on the time of occultation are plenty. In the narration of the scroll which was revealed to the Holy Prophet (s) mentioning the names of the Imams (a) after him, Imam Al-Mahdi (aj) is described after Imam Hasan Al-Askari (a),

> *He will then fulfill this matter by his son, a mercy to mankind. He will have the perfection of Moses, the glory of Jesus, and the patience of Job. My followers will be humiliated in his time, and their heads will roll just like the heads of the Turks and the Daylum. They will be killed, burnt, and terrorized. Their blood will stain the earth and their women will wail and cry. Those are indeed my followers. With them the greatest trials are repelled. With them earthquakes will be prevented, and binds and shackles removed. They are the one's who will have blessings and mercy from their Lord, and they are the guided ones.*[13]

There are also a number of similar noble traditions.

---

[12] The Holy Quran, 2:214.

[13] Al-Tabrasi, *I'lam Al-Wara bi-A'lam Al-Huda*, 393.

If the believers find themselves in difficult times, it is the promise of God that is fulfilled. That gives them greater foresight in their truth and faith in the certainty of their calling. God says in the Holy Quran,

> *But when the faithful saw the confederates, they said, 'This is what God and His Apostle had promised us, and God and His Apostle were true.' And it only increased them in faith and submission.*[14]

Thirdly, we must recall our deep history of patience and steadfastness on the truth, and persistence on taking to that same path of principles, throughout the various circumstances. We must also recall the success and fruit borne from this, such that others had no choice but to accept it as a force that must be acknowledged and worked with.

Fourthly, there must be an emphasis given to invitation and discourse, presenting different perspectives, and renewing the presentation of evidence that is suitable for our day and age. This must be done with open-mindedness and complete objectivity. Truth and honesty are critical, as well the avoidance of convoluted discussions, fallacies, and meaningless rhetoric. Like our Imams (a) have said, a little of truth will suffice over a lot of falsehood.[15]

Given that we possess an abundance of strong evidence and proof, sufficient for those who are fair-minded with intellect

---

[14] The Holy Quran, 33:22.
[15] Al-Mufid, *Al-Irshaad*, 2:199.

and insight, it should be known that "He who strays cannot hurt you if you are guided."[16]

Fifthly, we must protect and hold on to our symbols, rituals, and commemorations. We must continue to offer the teachings and beliefs of the Holy Household (a) and revive their cause. This has the greatest effect on the Shia coming together, becoming closer, deepening their understanding of their faith, and reviving their determination and steadfastness. It also grabs other people's attention and intrigues them. This is our protective shield and our success. Our Imams (a) emphasized this with us,[17] just as our history testifies to it.

Sixthly, we must unite in our ranks and in our speech. We must ease the tension of our differences and bring our perspectives closer to one another. We must rise above false allegations, name-calling, and petty accusations devoted to pushing one perspective over another or to create a buzz and attract attention.

Seventhly, we must greatly beware of invitations toward distorted creeds or defeatism (i.e. calls to compromise our beliefs and practices). This is an existential threat to the entity of Shiism and its teachings. These calls are suspicious ones, where their goal could be to circumvent the path of the Holy Progeny (a) while its followers are heedless to the reality of the call. In other words, they could be indirect campaigns

---

[16] The Holy Quran, 5:105.
[17] Al-Amili, *Wasai'l Al-Shia*, 10:392.

with agendas meant to distract and sway the followers away from the truth, without them realizing this.

Therefore, it is necessary to stand firmly against those calls and their callers, with determination and wisdom, alongside the virtuous scholars. It is because of the severity of such deviant calls that the Imams (a) stood firmly against them without compromise.

Of the most significant causes for protection from the deviant calls and the exposition of their falsehood, is the acquaintance with the greatest possible number of narrations from the Holy Prophet (s) and his Household (a). The narrations show us their true teachings and allow us to distinguish between guidance and misguidance. They allow us to detect deviance and protect ourselves from the threats of defeatism.

Of course, we do not allow violence as a way to respond to any threats whatsoever. Indeed, we are of God and to Him we shall return.

Finally, we must stress our connection to God, as well as our sincerity and service to Him. We hold on to Him, encompassed by His protection and care. He is the greatest supporter and the guardian of the believers. "Whoever takes for his guardians God, His Apostle and the faithful [should know that] the confederates of God are indeed the victorious."[18]

---

18 The Holy Quran, 5:56.

WHAT MAKES THE ISLAMIC SEMINARY UNIQUE

What are the most important features that distinguish the Islamic Seminary and the Marjaeya from the rest of the religious institutions from different faiths and schools of thought?

There are two primary distinguishing factors of the school of the Holy Household (a).

1) True education and beneficial knowledge – built on the emphasis of strong proofs, a high standard of scrutiny, and strong critique, for the purpose of reaching truth and realizing our religious obligations. The Imams (a), and their followers, were known for this from the earliest times. They stood out from the rest as this characteristic was evident in their teachings as well as their discussions, gatherings, and conduct.

2) Sincerity and devotion in seeking knowledge and understanding, with the purpose of fulfilling one's obligation and being relieved of liability before God – not to seek this world's pleasures, or to obtain positions of power or monetary wealth. The Imams (a) represent the peak of devotion to God and manifest His calling and remembrance. Their followers are enlightened by their light. They see with the rays of their torch. Their existence is completed by the blessings that flow from their sacred emanations.

This school has persevered with these two foundations, under the care and patronage of the Ahlulbayt (a).

This, of course, does not mean that there have not been problematic incidents, as that is only natural with the absence of the immaculate leadership of the Ahlulbayt. However, what we intend to convey here is that the general direction of the seminaries do not go outside of these two foundations, by the blessings of the Holy Household (a) and the protection of the Awaited Imam (aj). If a seminary was to fail in respect to either of these two foundations, it would be seen to fail in being recognized as a seminary and in delivering what is expected and anticipated from it.

The relationship between the believers and the seminaries was built and grew on the basis of spirituality and sacredness, such that the Marja has a special place in the hearts and souls of the believers. He was seen as a representative of the Imam (aj) – who is the embodiment of sanctity and holiness.

There are a few things that helped keep this relationship between the seminary and the people alive.

Firstly, the seminary's educational setup is quite unique. It does not mandate a particular system in seminary studies. Every individual is free to learn based on his own persuasion within the general seminary framework. No individual is forced into adopting a particular schedule, instructor, or course. The student of the seminary has complete autonomy in utilizing his skills and potential, just as he is responsible to fulfill his religious duties before God with due diligence and a clear conscience.

Secondly, the seminary is not subject to an authority that dictates the affairs of the seminary. There is no sole decision-making body that discerns who studies what subjects or who is allowed to climb the ranks of the seminary. From the introductory stages of study to the Marjaeya itself, seminarians are evaluated by a natural organic process of numerous individuals based on their own observations and interactions.

Thirdly, the seminary is financially independent from any government or body of influence. It generally relies on the religious dues paid by the believers who are fulfilling their religious duties, without imposing or making conditions in this regard either.

These characteristics – as well as the support of God and the patronage of the Imam of the Time (aj) – have had the greatest impact in preserving the seminaries' sanctity and glory, as well as on the development of the sciences within the seminary.

The scholars in the seminaries, distinguished in the depths of their knowledge and research, play an instrumental role in the academic status of the seminaries. They are honorable men known for their piety, ethics, and virtue. They impressed the people's hearts and minds, becoming a symbol of honor and pride for them.

The seminaries have an independent presence. Their movement was impactful and their voice was heard – although, in various circumstances and situations, others attempted to stifle and push it away.

It was very difficult, rather impossible, for governments and other powers to push the seminaries away from their course or sway them from their goals. They would try to limit the scope of study and scholastic development to mere ceremonial titles. Some wanted to circumvent the system and utilize it for illegitimate purposes. This behavior was seen from governmental agencies and bureaucracies, especially in underdeveloped countries.

In these ways that the Shia seminaries have distinguished themselves from other schools of thought and faiths. Of course, the seminaries are not void from defects and painful shortcomings.

Much potential and talent is wasted as a result of the freedom offered and lack of a set structure in seminary education. Though it allows for autonomy and free thinking, some do not maximize their time in studying or teaching, be it out of laziness or boredom, without an authority over them. In addition, some seminarians that are qualified to rise in the ranks do not do so because they are not seen – due to the absence of precise measures to provide assessments of individuals.

Furthermore, many individuals that are competent and qualified to take certain positions are not able to do so for the lack of official standardized assessments for qualification. Moreover, in the current open and autonomous setup of the seminary, the door is open for the possibility of individuals who are not qualified to step up and project themselves for people to follow.

Nevertheless, all of these negatives do not compare to the great gains and strides made by the seminary over such a long period of time in its establishment, solidarity, steadfastness, independence and influence.

It is possible to avoid much of the negatives or lessen the shortcomings, by focusing on the religious aspects within the seminary, as well as with the believers who work with it. Paying attention to the religious morals can prevent many of the shortcomings that take place, because they protect people's rights and emphasize upholding one's responsibility – in seeking knowledge and propagating it – in the best manner. Thus, focusing on this is one of the most important obligations. God said, "Admonish, for admonition indeed benefits the faithful."[19]

The seminaries have had to play many roles and capacities leading to much hardship and trial, and even great tragedies. It is not easy for governments and other powers to infiltrate these seminaries and disband the independence of these institutions and their active impact on society. Yet, the struggle remains and we do not see an end in sight. So we carry on knowing that our support is from God alone, the best of supporters.

---

[19] The Holy Quran, 51:55.

INTRAFAITH AND INTERFAITH

WITH OTHER SCHOOLS OF THOUGHT AND BEING OPEN TO THEM

How do you look at working with and opening up to other schools of thought within Islam?

Working with other schools of thought is definitely a good and positive step that the Holy Household (a) themselves adopted. The reality that we face mandates that we do so, for the enemies of the path of the Household (a) also oppose Islam in its general sense. Just as it is a duty for us to defend the line of the Household (a), it is our duty to defend Islam in the general sense as well.

Our Imams (a) set the greatest examples for us as they sacrificed their own rights to safeguard and protect Islam. The

Commander of the Faithful (a) did not pursue his rights because he feared for Islam's disintegration. In fact, he did not hesitate to serve the body of Islam by providing counsel to those in governance, supporting them, and working with them.

Imam Al-Baqir (a) rescued those at the helm during a humiliating position faced with the minting of currency during his lifetime.[1] Many years later, Imam Al-Askari (a) was put in a similar situation when the Abbasid caliph Al-Mutawakkil asked him for help with the drought they faced and the ongoing claims of the Christians regarding the disaster, even though the Imam (a) was imprisoned at the time.[2] Furthermore, our Imams (a) granted their followers permission to fight in the Muslim army along the borders of the nation to defend the Muslim nation.[3]

Following suit, our scholars continued with similar positions time after time. They supported the Ottomans, who the Shia saw only the worst from, and raised in arms with them to defend the body of Islam. This would earn them the ire of colonial powers who came to control the land and the future of its people.

In the not too distant past, my grandfather the late Sayyid Al-Hakeem opened doors of cooperation and collaboration with the other sects in Iraq. This was done during his tenure in

---

[1] Al-Demyari, *Hayat Al-Hayawan*, 1:114.
[2] Al-Arbali, *Kashf Al-Ghumma*, 2:429.
[3] Al-Amili, *Wasai'l Al-Shia*, 11:19.

standing against the spread of communism and atheism in the region.

It may be said that these positions show a lack of depth and cunningness. This is a quick way to suppress reality, but is the cost that must be paid for principled realism. It is much like what was said before – that "Muawiya is more cunning than Ali (a)."[4]

Back to the original discussion, engaging with other schools of thought in Islam is definitely a great thing for the sake of protecting the body of Islam. It is not only a positive behavior, it is especially necessary in our day and age.

Of course, we must be mindful to hold true to our creed and our principles. We should never compromise our faith for the sake of easing our relationship with others. It would be meaningless to compromise the soul of Islam and its reality for the sake of protecting its existence. That would be contradictory. Our Imams (a) would emphasize calling toward truth wherever it was appropriate and effective. This was done throughout their mission, as they worked for the protection of the faith and its principles.

Of course, such compromise is not necessary for the sake of cooperation for the service of Islam. That is, unless the other side is stubborn in its extremism such that they do not care for the general wellbeing of Islam. If this were the case, then

---

[4] Al-Radi, *Nahjul Balagha*, Sermon 200.

cooperation should not be a goal, as it would be a great detriment to Islam and Muslims. "Indeed God is the All-sufficient, the All-laudable."[5]

THE RIGHT WAY FOR MUSLIMS TO WORK TOGETHER

> *What is the correct way for Muslims to live, work, and deal with one another?*

Muslims must live amongst each other in tolerance and mutual respect. Each person's rights must be respected and honored. Thereafter, the following points should remembered:

1) Each side must seek to understand the other, by learning their beliefs and ideas from the sources that they acknowledge and identify with. At the same time, they should get to know one another by coexisting and interacting with each other. Moreover, they must dispel the preconceived notions that have developed over time as a result of bigotry, extremism, and stereotypes, whether they have developed knowingly or subconsciously.

2) All sides must present themselves and their perspectives intellectually and with full context. Let discourse and dialogue take place on this basis. Avoid vilifying,

---

[5] The Holy Quran, 22:64.

defaming, mocking, and insulting others. Such reactionary methods do not help protect the body of Islam, they only go forth to weaken it and make it more vulnerable.

3) The ideas of all sides should be broadcasted – be it in creed, jurisprudence, civics, history, or other subjects – using all media platforms available. Let everyone see what the others have to offer.

4) Every person should be given the freedom to choose whatever creed or ideas to adopt within the general framework of Islam, without being coerced into accepting someone else's beliefs or giving up his or her own. Of course, there is no problem with civil discourse concerning religious realities, achieving salvation, and clearing our obligations toward God Almighty.

5) In every school of thought, there should be people who vocally denounce anyone who does not act in accordance to the etiquettes we described here. Thus, those who do not follow suit will be pressured within their own school to conform to civil discourse and coexistence. People will then be able to clearly distinguish between right and wrong in these matters.

DIALOGUE WITH OTHER FAITHS, PARTICULARLY CHRISTIANITY

How do you view dialogue with other faiths, particularly the Christian faith?

With the advancement of technology and the means of communication, such that the world has become as intertwined as an individual city, all should be understanding of one another, and the doors to open dialogue should be open, for the best interests of all parties, their peaceful coexistence, and doing away with the obstacles arising from differences in faith, nationality, and ideology.

This speaks true especially with our engagement with the other Abrahamic faiths – who share in the divine truth. They all call for ethics and setting the right moral example. Likewise, they are all equally threatened by the movement of materialism and immorality that conflicts with each faith's ethics and moral code. They are threatened by the evil forces that call for disbelief in the unseen and abandonment of ideals and ethics, thereby eliminating mankind's humanity and instilling in us only the bestial and vile.

We emphasize this in particular between the two largest faiths in the world – Islam and Christianity. They are in the greatest need for dialogue and cooperation, especially with the overlapping interests between Muslims and Christians across the globe and their coexistence with one another.

The importance of this was finally illuminated through the cooperation between the Marjayea and the Vatican. This cooperation has resulted in a number of important accomplishments in the face of attempts to undermine ethics and morality.

THE MARJAEYA AND COLONIALISM

COMBATTING COLONIALISM

> *The Marjaeya has a deep history in combatting colonialism. Could you shed some light and provide some detail with regards to some of the stances of the Marjaeya in this regard?*

The Marjaeya's opposition and combatting of colonialism is an extension of the principled stances of Shiism that the Holy Household (a) emphasized through their teachings and their own conduct. They emphasized putting aside our differences as Muslims when Islam is being threatened and face our common enemy to protect the body of Islam. For submission to the religion comes before faith in the true school of thought, because the latter would not be known nor would an individual reach it before knowing the religion itself.

The Commander of the Faithful (a) set this example. Though his rights were stripped away from him and he was oppressed by those who usurped his political authority, he remained patient and resilient. He secluded himself from them, took a position against them, and did not pay allegiance. When the religion of Islam was exposed to the danger of disintegration he was forced, however, to give allegiance under duress for the purpose of protecting the body of Islam. Imam Ali (a) said,

> *I withheld my hand till I saw that many people were reverting from Islam and were calling for the destruction of the religion of Muhammad (s). I then feared that if I did not protect Islam and its people, and there occurred in it a breach or destruction, it would mean a greater blow to me than the loss of power over you which was, in any case, to last for a few days.... Therefore, in these happenings I rose until wrong was destroyed, and religion attained peace and safety.*[1]

The Imams (a) after Imam Ali (a) lived during the reign of tyrants. Fighting in the battles of the conquests they launched was forbidden, because they did not abide by the religious guidelines in those wars. To fight for them would be to be support them. However, the Imams (a) ordered that Muslims fight – not for the ruling authorities but to protect the religion of Islam.

It is narrated that Imam Al-Rida (a) said,

---

[1] Al-Radi, *Nahjul Balagha*, Letter 62 (To the people of Egypt sent through Malik Al-Ashtar when he was appointed as its governor).

One will take his position and will not fight. If he fears for Islam and his fellow Muslims, he fights. His fight would be for himself, not the ruling authority. It is because in the erasure of Islam is the erasure of the remembrance of Muhammad (s).[2]

In a narration by Imam Al-Sadiq (a) he said,

It is upon a Muslim to hold himself and fight for the rule of God and the rule of His Messenger. But to fight the disbelievers for the sake of tyrannical rule and their tradition — that is not permissible.[3]

Our great Maraje and scholars followed through with the example set by our Imams (a). While they separate themselves from oppressive regimes and condemn them, and those regimes take positions at odds with the Marjaeya and the believers, sometimes the Marjaeya is forced to call the people to stand with the government when it is attacked by foreign aggression to protect the Islam as a whole and the lives of Muslims.

If they are successful, they are not appreciated. If they fail, even if it is due to the lack of strategy and implementation by the government, they bear the burden of failure. There is no recourse for them except the pleasure of God, relieving themselves of their responsibilities before God with due diligence, and always pursuing His straight path.

---

[2] Al-Amili, *Wasai'l Al-Shia*, Vol. 11, Ch. 6 of Jihad Al-Adu, Tr. 2.

[3] Ibid, Tr. 3

The stances of our scholars against foreign aggression come in a number of different ways. They all are joined by the common purpose of not bowing to disbelief, but instead standing up to it, and preventing it from harming Islam to the greatest extent possible. There are three primary stances in this.

The Ideological Stance

The Marjaeya and our scholars have pushed forward the resources of the seminary to clarify the truths of the faith. They have worked to debunk the incorrect accusations against the religion, whether they originated in the lands of Muslims or elsewhere.

The stances against missionaries, utilized by colonizers to subjugate Muslim populations, is a key example. One of the thought-leaders in this regard was the late Ayatollah Shaykh Muhammad Jawad Al-Balaghi,[4] a renowned scholar and author of many important publications.

Similar firm stances were taken against the spread of communism later in the century, as we have discussed previously.

The Military Stance

In more recent times where Islamic governments were weakened and foreign advancements in Muslim countries increased, the position of Muslims – as both governments and

---

[4] Ayatollah Shaykh Muhammad Jawad Al-Shaykh Hassan Al-Balaghi (1280 – 1352 AH) was an esteemed jurist in the Islamic Seminary of the Holy City of Najaf. He was a strong proponent of creed, spoke a few foreign languages, and was a great poet. Some of his publications included *Aalaa Al-Rahman fi Tafseer Al-Quran, Al-Huda ila Deen Al-Mustafa,* and *Al-Rihla Al-Madrasiya.*

people – was one of a defensive nature. The scholars played an important role in this in a number of occasions.

In the mid-13th Hijri century (or 1941 CE), the Russians invaded Iran. The scholars of Iran came out to defend their homeland alongside the fighters. One of the most prominent figures then was the Marja Ayatollah Shaykh Ahmad Al-Naraqi.[5] The late Sayyid Muhammad Al-Mujahid ibn Al-Sayyid Sahib Al-Riyadh was also a strong proponent of the stance against the Russian invasion. He left Karbala, and encouraged those with him to do the same, to aid the opposition against the Russians. Their stance was valiant and victory would have been their ally, if it were not for the number of betrayals and mismanagement in the Iranian military. The betrayal and mismanagement led to Russian occupation of Azerbaijan and other parts of Iran. They endured the loss and the sharp criticism of the ignorant.

In the beginning of the of the 14th Hijri century, the Russians attacked Iran again and controlled some of its territory. The Italians also attacked Tripoli in the west. Our scholars issued the edict that it was obligatory to unite in resistance of foreign occupation of Muslim land. One of those scholars was the great Marja Sayyid Muhammad Kadhim Al-Tabatabaei Al-Yazdi.

---

[5] Ayatollah Shaykh Ahmad Al-Shaykh Muhammad Mahdi Al-Naraqi (1185 – 1245 AH) was one of the Maraje in Iran. He completed his religious education in the Islamic Seminary of Najaf and settled in Iran thereafter. One of his most notable publications was *Mustanad Al-Shia fi Ahkam Al-Sharee'a*.

In Iran, the late Al-Akhound Ayatollah Shaykh Muhammad Kadhim Al-Khurasani[6] would prepare himself and his people for battle. He even made his travel arrangements and was ready to move out, along with a group of scholars of his time. However, the late Akhound's sudden death unraveled those plans. Indeed, God carries through whatever He wishes.

When the British armies invaded Iraq during their war with the Ottomans, the Shia and their scholars did not side with the British against the Ottomans. Note that the Shia saw nothing but oppression, subjugation, tyranny and ignorance at the hands of the Ottoman Empire. The Ottomans did not even acknowledge the Ja'fari[7] school of thought. In any rulings pertaining to the Shia, the state imposed Hanafi jurisprudence on them. They imposed their rules and policies forcefully and had no consideration for the Shia community or their scholars. Shia scholars were not excused from military service, regardless of their knowledge or status.

Yet with all of this, our scholars put it all aside and made it a priority to uphold their duty in protecting Islam and defending their faith. There were two fronts that they fought on: the regions of Al-Shu'ayba and Al-Kout. Amongst these scholars

---

[6] Ayatollah Shaykh Muhammad Kathim ibn Al-Mulla Hussain Al-Akhound Al-Khurasani (1255 – 1329 AH) became the Marja of his time in the Holy City of Najaf. He was a staunch Usooli. Some of his most notable publications were *Kifayet Al-Usool, Hashiyet Al-Asfar,* and *Hashiyet Fara'id Al-Usool.*

[7] There are five widely accepted jurisprudential schools of thought in Islam, four of which are Sunni (Hanbali, Shafi'i, Hanafi, and Maliki) and one of which is Shia – the Ja'fari school. – Eds.

were Sayyid Muahmmad Saeed Al-Haboubi[8] with my grandfather Sayyid Al-Hakeem who was a young man at the time.
In addition, there was Shaykh Al-Sharee'a Al-Asfahani, Sayyid Ali Al-Damad, Sayyid Abulqassim Al-Kashani, Sayyid
Mahdi Al-Haydari, Shaykh Mahdi Al-Khalissi, and many others.[9]

---

[8] Sayyid Muhammad Saeed Al-Sayyid Mahmoud Al-Haboubi (1266 – 1333 AH)
was a great jurist from the Holy City of Najaf. He was widely regarded as of the
top poets of the Arabic language during his time. He was a champion of the people given his sacrifice and struggle for the faith. He has numerous writings in
jurisprudence and the principles of jurisprudence, as well as poetry.

[9] The following are brief biographies of each of the scholars named above:
Shaykh Fathallah Al-Shaykh Muhammad Jawad Al-Asfahani (1266 – 1339 AH),
known as Shaykh Al-Sharee'a, was one of the great jurists of the seminary of the
Holy City of Najaf. He was brilliant in the principles of jurisprudence, mathematics, and other abstract sciences. He was a true fighter. He took on the leadership
role of fighting against the English after the passing of Shaykh Muhammad Taqi
Al-Shirazi. When the English invaded the Holy City of Najaf, the people left him.
He was besieged in his home until he died. Some of his most notable publications
include *Qa'idet La Dharar* and *Qa'idet Al-Wahid Al-Baseet La Yasdur Minh Illa Wahid*.
Sayyid Ali Al-Sayyid Muhammad Al-Damad (1275 – 1336 AH) was one of the
jurists of the Islamic Seminary in the Holy City of Najaf. He sacrificed much in
his struggle to defend the faith on the battlefield. After the Muslim armies were
pushed back, he returned to the Holy City of Najaf deeply hurt. A British recon-
naissance plane flew over the city one day. When he heard the sound of the air-
craft he was deeply hurt and sobbed profusely. He passed away very soon after.
Some of his most notable publications include *Taqreerat Al-Usool* and *Mishbah Al-
Thalam fi Shara'i Al-Islam*.
Sayyid Abulqassim Al-Sayyid Mustafa Al-Kashani (~1300 – 1381 AH) was one of
the great scholars in Iraq. He was selected by the people in Baghdad and
Kathimiya, along with other brave leaders, to represent them in negotiating with
the occupiers on vital political matters. He worked with other grand scholars such
as Shaykh Muhammad Jawad Al-Jaza'iri and Sayyid Hebatuddine Al-Shahristani,
during the military operations on the battle fronts of Hilla and Tuwayreej. His
valiant stances and motivational speeches were instrumental in rallying fighters to
defend their land and strengthening morale amongst the soldiers. The English
pursued him after the occupation. Thus, he fled to Iran and lived there for years
before he passed.
Sayyid Mahdi Al-Sayyid Ahmad Al-Haydari passed away in 1336 AH. He was a
Marja in the Holy City of Kathimiya. Along with his sons and other scholars at
his side, he came out to the people of Baghdad and other surrounding cities and

Sayyid Muhammad Kadhim Al-Tabatabaei Al-Yazdi[10] and Shaykh Muhammad Taqi Al-Shirazi[11] - the two other grand scholars – also sent their sons Sayyid Muhammad[12] and Shaykh Muhammad Ridha[13] forward to support the revolution.

---

tribes to rally them for revolution and fighting against the foreign occupation. He was present at the battles of Al-Qarna, Al-Shu'ayba, and Al-Kowt. One of the Sayyid's most notable publications was *Ta'leeq 'ala Fara'id Al-Usool.*

Shaykh Mahdi Al-Shaykh Muhammad Hussain Al-Khalissi (1276 – 1343 AH) was a Marja in the Holy City of Kathimiya. He fought the English alongside the other brave scholars, and would then return to expose the corrupt politicians that followed. He was exiled to Hijaz (western coastal region of modern-day Saudi Arabia that includes the holy cities of Mecca and Medina) and for a period of time to Iran. He died a stranger, with little to no one by his side. Some of his most notable publications include *Al-Sharee'a Al-Samhaa', Al-Qawa'id Al-Fiqhiyya,* and *Kitab Al-Rijal.*

In addition to these scholars, there were the likes of Shaykh Abdulkarim Al-Jaza'iri, our grandfather the late Sayyid Muhammad Saeed Al-Hakeem, Shaykh Abdulridha Al-Shaykh Al-Radhi, Shaykh Jawad Al-Jawahiri, Shaykh Rahoom Al-Thalimi, Sayyid Abdulrazzaq Al-Helou, Shaykh Baqir Haydar, Shaykh Ja'far Al-Shaykh Al-Radhi, and others.

[10] Sayyid Muhammad Kathim Al-Sayyid Abdulatheem Al-Yazdi (1247 – 1337 AH) was led the Islamic Seminary in the Holy City of Najaf. He was entrenched in the sciences of jurisprudence and the principles of jurisprudences. Some of his most notable publications include *Al-Urwa Al-Wuthqa, Ijtimaa' Al-Amr wal-Nahi,* and *Al-Istishab.*

[11] Shaykh Muhammad Taqi ibn Al-Mirza Muhib Ali Al-Shirazi (1270 – 1338 AH) was one of the Maraje widely regarded in both seminaries of Karbala and Najaf. He was an esteemed writer and poet, as well as a valiant fighter and staunch defender of the faith. He led the Iraqi revolution against the English and triggered its first movements. Some of his most notable works include *Sharh Makasib Al-Shaykh Al-Ansari, Al-Aqaid Al-Fakhira fi Madh Al-Aqeeda Al-Tahira,* and *Risala fi Ahkam Al-Khalal.*

[12] Sayyid Muhammad Al-Sayyid Muhammad Kathim Al-Yazdi passed away in 1334 AH. He was a teacher of jurisprudence and the principles of jurisprudence at the Islamic Seminary of the Holy City of Najaf. He took part in the revolution and fought against the English. Some of his works include *Kitab Al-Hajj* and *Al-Kashkoul.*

[13] He was one of the most notable sons of the Iraqi revolution. He had a widely recognized role in mobilizing the masses in standing to fight against the English. He organized a huge event in the courtyards of the Shrines of Imam Al-Hussain

The Ottoman government offered sums of money to the scholars to be used at the time of war. The scholars refused. Their dignity and honor was far more important. Likewise, they were adamant on keeping their purpose purely for God and upholding their duty towards their faith. They say that Sayyid Al-Haboubi was content with eating dates as his only meal, as well as sitting and sleeping on the bare floor.

As the battles ensued the Turkish army proved to betray their allegiances quickly. Their betrayals and lack of management caused the military campaign at Al-Shu'ayba to fail. The scholars that survived were forced to retreat, knowing that they had upheld their duty. Sayyid Al-Haboubi said after returning, "Praise be to God who allowed me to uphold my duty."

Still, they were so deeply pained when they saw the foreign occupier have victory over the Muslims, enter their lands and wreak corruption. Many of the scholars fell to sorrow and became very ill, like Sayyid Al-Haboubi. He died in Nasiriya. He would be taken to the Holy City of Najaf for his funeral and burial.

On the Al-Kout front victory was realized, but was short-lived. The British forces were able to regain the territory that they lost after the Ottomans in Iraq were further disrupted.

---

and Al-Abbas in the Holy City of Karbala. Thousands of people showed up calling for resistance and protest against English occupation. He rallied troops from numerous cities across Iraq. He fought against the English in the battle of Al-Qarna. He was pursued by the occupiers in Karbala and exiled to India. His capture and exile played a big role in fueling the fire of the revolution against the occupation across Iraq.

Soon after this, the English were able to occupy all of Iraq and the Ottomans retreated.

When the British entrenched their influence and occupied Iraq, our scholars did not wait long before demanding that they free Iraq and grant it its independence. When the British continued to ignore their requests, the scholars launched a revolution that would become known as Thawrat Al-Ashreen,[14] led by the Marja Shaykh Muhammad Taqi Al-Shirazi. The late Shaykh Al-Sharee'a Al-Asfahani would eventually succeed him as leader of the revolution.

They carried out their duty and fulfilled their obligations. They endured the greatest hardships. They were besieged, terrorized, imprisoned, and exiled. They struggled in the way of their Lord, stood by their principles, and carried out the duties as they saw it.

---

[14] Thawrat Al-Ashreen was one of the greatest revolutions in Iraq's contemporary history, ignited by the religious scholars in 1920 against English occupation in Iraq. The scholars sacrificed much in this revolution as they defended Islam and the Muslims. With the leadership of our scholars, the valiant fighters of the revolution were distributed across numerous battle fronts to face the occupation. As told by English politicians, over the period of five months from the beginning of July in 1920 — every four hours one soldier was killed, 16 soldiers went missing, and 266 sterling pounds were spent every 24 hours. Phillip Willard Ireland reports this in his 1937 publication, *Iraq: A Study in Political Development*. From a political perspective Naji Shawket states, "In our belief if it were not for this great Iraqi revolution, Iraq would not have been able to achieve anything that even looks like independence. It would have been able to become a nation amongst the nations of the world, some of which wished to prevent it from achieving its statehood. But Iraq would be the first independent Arab state to sit amongst world nations. In a time that no Arab nation even dreamed of independence, such nations are indebted to Iraq for its revolution…" (*Al-Thikrayat*, 56). Contemporary historians point out that it is these jurists and scholars, the leaders in central Mesopotamia, as well as the leaders of the national movement in Baghdad that are truly the founders of modern-day Iraq and not the commonly offered political names.

They did not stop at that. As the new national government of Iraq was being formed under the British rule, Faisal I was called on to be its monarch, and our scholars would demand that the rights of Islam and Muslims be honored and protected. They wanted to make sure that Britain and its loyalists would not take the people for granted and thus stressed the rights of the people. However, they did. The scholars were forbidden from participating from the general referendums conducted, but still they remained firm to their stance in advocating for the rights of Islam and Muslims.

The new government took a harsh stance against the scholars. They exiled a number of them, including the late Shaykh Mahdi Al-Khalissi of Kadhimiya. The scholars of the Holy City of Najaf stood along his side. The two Grand Ayatollahs, Mirza Muhammad Hussain Al-Na'eeni and Sayyid Abulhassan Al-Asfahani[15] warned that they would leave the country if Shaykh Al-Khalissi was not brought back home.

The government did not respond and they did not bring back the Shaykh. Thus, the two Grand Ayatollahs followed through with their promise and left the country. They were joined by a massive group of scholars when they moved to Iran. They left at a very tense time in Iraq. The religious presence of scholars in Iraq was weakened, while irreligious rhetoric and missionaries took to the field. The purpose was to

---

[15] Ayatollah Sayyid Abulhassan Al-Sayyid Muhammad Al-Asfahani (1284 – 1365 AH) was great jurist and a Marja of his time. He was highly regarded for his support for organizations focused on religious education and awareness. Some of his most notable publications include *Sirat Al-Najat, Hashiyet Al-Urwa Al-Wuthqa,* and *Waseelet Al-Najat.*

strip people away from their religious identity. The foreign occupiers wanted to weaken the threat of the religious establishment in both Iraq and Iran, as well as in the surrounding Muslim nations. The less people's attachment was to religion, the better it was for the designs of colonialism and foreign occupation. Our scholars knew this.

Sayyid Ahmad, the son of the Marja Ayatollah Sayyid Jamal Al-Hashimi,[16] spoke to me about his father's experience in moving to Iran. His father was one of the close students of Al-Mirza Al-Na'eeni. He was with him during the group's move to Iran. Sayyid Al-Hashimi describes their entrance into the neighboring nation, "When the scholars traveled to Iran, the Iranian people and their scholars welcomed them with a huge warm welcoming. They celebrated them, praised them, and honored them."

When Al-Mirza Al-Na'eeni saw the Iranian people's care and affection for them, he told the scholars, "We can, by what we see of the people's rush towards us, better the situation here in Iran." The late Marja Ayatollah Shaykh Abdulkareem Al-Haeri Al-Yazdi[17] said to him, "We are meeting a mountain of

---

[16] Sayyid Jamal Al-Sayyid Hussain Al-Gulpaygani (1295 – 1377 AH) was a Marja from the Holy City of Najaf and an esteemed professor of jurisprudence and principles of jurisprudence. He was born in the village of Saeedabad and passed away in the Holy City of Najaf. Some of his most notable publications include *Al-Ijtihad wat-Taqleed, Jawaz Al-Baqaa' ala Taqleed Al-Mayyit,* and *Thakheeret Al-Ibad li-youm Al-Ma'aad.*

[17] Shaykh Abdulkareem ibn Al-Mawla Muhammad Ja'far Al-Haeri (1276 – 1355 AH) established what is the current Islamic Seminary of Qum in Iran. He supervised the instruction of the seminary students and established a rigorous curriculum with an annual examination to assess their level and progress. He administered the affairs of the Marjaeya with wisdom and grace during a turbulent time.

tribulation. It is not for us but to be quiet and to preserve what remains until this tribulation passes…"

It was as if he was seeing with the light of God. What he predicted came true, because soon after Ridha Pahlavi would become the monarch of Iran. He scorched the fabric of society and tried to uproot faith from people's lives, which was seen in a series of tribulations experienced by the scholars and the believers.

Those who remained in the Holy City of Najaf found that a big void had been created. They realized the danger at stake and the necessity for the scholars to come back to their positions and renew the activity and functions of the seminary. They knew that the scholars had to preserve what was left of the religion after they were unable to reform the institution of rule and government in Iraq.

They pursued bringing the scholars back. One of the individuals who took this on and tirelessly worked for this goal was the late Ayatollah Shaykh Baqir Al-Qamousi.[18] His son, Shaykh Sadiq Al-Qamousi,[19] spoke to me in great detail about his father's experiences.

Some of his most notable publications include *Durar Al-Usool, Kitab Al-Salat,* and *Al-Taqreerat.*

[18] Ayatollah Shaykh Baqir Al-Qamousi was one of the great jurists of the Islamic Seminary of the Holy City of Najaf. He taught in the seminary and was known for his piety, wisdom, humility and impeccable moral character.

[19] Shaykh Sadiq Al-Qamousi was a scholar known for his piety, prudence, and ethics. He was also regarded as a brilliant poet. He had a number of commentaries on books of jurisprudence and principles of jurisprudence.

Some scholars disagreed with Shaykh Baqir, and saw that if they were to return to Iraq without having their demands met it would be a show of weakness. Nonetheless, he continued to emphasize the need for their return. He clarified that the circumstances were dire and beseeched his relationships with the scholars. Eventually he was successful. Many of the scholars, and those who left with them, returned to Iraq. They renewed their activities in the seminary and focused on further development, away from friction with the authorities and government.

It worked out very well this way, because soon after the seminaries in Iraq would become a safe haven for those who would flee the ironclad Pahlavi rule. Pahlavi's suppression of the religious establishment in Iran looked like a type of vengeance against the scholars. Those who were able to escape Iran from the tyrannical rule would seek out the seminaries in Iraq as a sanctuary. The Iranian regime was aware of this and did not like it. Still, in Qum the late Ayatollah Shaykh Abdulkareem Al-Haeri Al-Yazdi would only deal with the situation with the utmost patience and prudence. Though the regime was ruthless, the Ayatollah's forbearance and leadership gave the religious community some breathing room.

Accordingly, both the seminaries of Iraq and Qum were both strengthened. Some of the greatest scholars would come from these seminaries. These establishments were at the forefront of protecting the faith as its impenetrable shield and vibrant voice.

The call of God was honored. The scholars upheld their duty in serving the people with this call and may God reward them the best of rewards. "All command belongs to God, before this and hereafter,"[20] and He is the guardian of the believers and the best of supporters. "Yet it may be that you dislike something, which is good for you…"[21] This is how the seminaries and the Marjaeya carried out their responsibilities in standing against foreign occupation and spoiling their plans that would have created even further damage.

In Turkey, on the other hand, the situation was quite different. The Marjaeya and the Shia generally had no voice to be heard. They had no reach or influence to preserve the integrity of the faith and the practice of it in society. Turkey turned from being a country that held the banner of Islam and one that would be the seat of the caliphate for the Muslim world for hundreds of years, to a new secular state that opposed Islam. It became a state that would call on to foreigners, in humiliation and indignity, for help and support.

Those who did not support this and its associated movements of reform were not feeble or meek. They did not betray their responsibility or take it lightly. They had a different perspective. They saw the strength of the enemy they faced and the material weakness that they themselves had.

In addition to this was the lack of established individuals of foresight and principle. There were too many individuals who

---

20 The Holy Quran, 30:4.
21 The Holy Quran, 2:216.

were weak in their resolve and selfish in their ambition – these individuals were likely to take control of the reform movement and steer it in the direction of their own personal interests and ambitions.

Ayatollah Sayyid Muhammad Kadhim Al-Tabatabaei Al-Yazdi chose not to fight the British and participate in the revolution after it declined militarily – because he was convinced that they could not win against the British in that way. British forces had taken over the country militarily and their influence had gone deep across the region.

Likewise, Sayyid Al-Yazdi held a similar position prior to this when he turned down the invitation to participate in drafting the new Iranian constitution – what would be known as *Al-Mashrouta*. He believed that the plans of reform by those who invited him would not be realized. He stated,

> *If the Shah is one wolf, then we will fall in the hands of seventy wolves. The people that we see siding with us and rushing towards us, will leave us as soon as their interests are threatened.*

To each is his own perspective, and it is each person's right to hold on to that and act accordingly. "Indeed, man is a witness to himself."[22] Deeds are in their intentions, and for every person is what he intends. God Almighty is the witness, and He is the source of all blessings.

---

[22] The Holy Quran, 75:14.

In Lebanon, the late Ayatollah Sayyid Abdulhussain Sharafeddine[23] took an honorable stance against French colonialism in his own homeland after the First World War. He reflected the same position as the Marjaeya did in Iraq against the British in Thawrat Al-Ashreen and what transpired thereafter. The French wished vengeance for his insurgence. They ordered that he be executed. The French forces attacked his home, burned his library to the ground, and transgressed against his rights and the rights of the believers with him. Enduring such hardship and sacrificing much for the principles long-held by the Marjaeya, he managed to escape from the French authorities into Palestine.

The late Ayatollah Sayyid Abulqassim Al-Kashani had some of the most inspiring stances against British presence in Iran after the Second World War. The primary outcome of his positions was the nationalization of Iranian oil after it had been primarily overtaken by British Petroleum.

Though the positions in the latter two events did not involve the leading Marjaeya of their times directly, they aligned and coincided with the general disposition and objectives of the Marjaeya.

---

[23] Ayatollah Sayyid Abdulhussain Yousef Charafeddine (1290 -1377 AH) was a Marja in Lebanon and a prominent national leader. He was highly regarded in the scientific, religious, political and social arenas. He stood valiantly and fought against French colonialism in Lebanon after the fall of the Ottoman Empire. In addition, he famously engaged in a discourse with Azhar University's Shaykh Saleem Al-Beshri, in what would become known as Al-Muraja'at. Some of the Sayyid's most notable publications are *Al-Fusool Al-Muhimma*, *Al-Nass wal-Ijtihad*, and *Al-Muraja'at*.

The honorable scholars and the Marjaeya had a series of positions against the infiltration of Zionism and its campaign to establish its state in Palestine. These stances began with the visit of the late Ayatollah Shaykh Muhammad Hussain Kashif Al-Ghita'[24] to Jerusalem. The purpose of his visit was to participate in an Islamic conference, which took place in the mid-14th Hijri century. His trip was conducted on behalf of the Marjaeya and supported by the scholars of the seminary. Even Al-Mirza Al-Na'eeni would see him off as he left the Holy City of Najaf. My grandfather the late Sayyid Al-Hakeem would do the same until he reached Baghdad. To this day, the positions and edicts in this regard are highly regarded.

The Negative Stance

What has made the Shia school of thought unique in all of its roles and positions is its refusal to submit to oppressors, based on the teachings of the Imams (a). Many groups deal with the challenges they face on the ground by acknowledging the oppressors or tyrants that oppress them, even if only superficially. Such admittance or acknowledgment can only give credence to the ongoing situation and bolster the presence of an oppressor. This school of thought, however, has

---

[24] Shaykh Muhammad Hussain Al-Shaykh Ali Kashif Al-Ghataa' (1294 – 1373 AH) was one of the great scholars and orators of his time. He lived and passed in the Holy City of Najaf. He fought against English colonialism in Iraq. The Shaykh also notably participated in numerous Arabic and Islamic conferences. Much of his work was published in publications across the Middle East. Moreover, he has a vast library established in his name. Some of his most prominent works include *Asl Al-Shia wa Usooliha, Tahreer Al-Majalla,* and *Al-Mathal Al-Ulya fil Islam la fi Bhamdoun.*

made it jurisprudentially forbidden to assist or submit to oppressors. Such acts are considered to be of the greater sins.
In fact, if all the believers were to take heed of these rulings,
the conditions of the Muslims would be much different.

The Marjaeya and the seminaries work in accordance to this
principle. They emphasized their independence and autonomous presence within society and outside of government.
Given that this is the position held when it comes to Muslim
governments, living under their rule, there is no doubt that
the Marjaeya would hold an even stronger position when it
comes to foreign governments that wish to impose their rule
on Muslims and subjugate them to their own interests. This
has been especially clear in recent history where foreign powers have attempted to increase their influence in Muslim nations. There are a number of incidents to point to in this regard.

The famous tobacco *fatwa* (edict) is one such example.[25] The
Iranian government had given the British exclusive rights to

---

[25] Nasseriddine Shah gave an English tobacco company exclusive rights to mo-
nopolize the Iranian tobacco industry. The lease for growing, valuation, and sell-
ing was signed for a fifty-year term to begin in 1890. The agreement had a very
negative impact on the domestic economy and its local markets. People took to
the streets in a popular revolt that year led by the scholars. Sayyid Al-Shirazi Al-
Kabeer sent numerous letters to the Shah of Iran demanding that he answer the
people's grievances and make the necessary change. However, his requests fell on
deaf ears. At that point, Sayyid Al-Shirazi issued his famous fatwa making it haram
(impermissible) to smoke tobacco. The Iranian people heeded to his verdict and
did not smoke. It is said that even the women of the Shah's royal palace stopped
smoking in the palace. With the people's resilience, the Shah was eventually forced
to concede to their demands and rescinded the contract with the British company
and refunded it its losses.

the nation's tobacco. Sayyid Al-Shirazi Al-Kabeer[26] realized how grave of a mistake that was, and that it would serve as a precursor to British power and influence in Iran, as it had with other nations. The Sayyid disrupted those plans by issuing his famous fatwa banning tobacco. The entire industry of tobacco in Iran basically shut down and brought great losses for the British company.

They tried to convince him to retract his edict and change his position. They promised him power and wealth. They guaranteed that anything he wished for could be realized if he would just withdraw the edict. After the delegation that was sent to meet him in Samarra finished presenting their overtures he said, "If you were to fill this whole world with gold and silver for me, I will not change my position."[27] He would not bend and the boycott would remain. It ended with the Shah conceding to the people's demands and rescinding the agreement with the British.

Another example of such positions also took place during Sayyid Al-Shirazi's time in Samarra, Iraq. Violence was on the

---

[26] Sayyid Muhammad Hassan Al-Sayyid Mahmoud Al-Shirazi (1230 – 1312 AH) was the Marja of his time. He migrated with a large group of scholars to Samarra, Iraq where he opened the doors of research, learning, and education there. He led in public affairs and cared deeply for the poor and underprivileged. He would bring them whatever they needed in clothing and food twice each and every year. Moreover, the Sayyid gave particular attention to the general social and political situation facing Muslims in different nations. He held a special council of experts and intellectuals that would convene whenever necessary to address the political challenges that Muslim communities faced at the time. Some of his notable publications include *Hashiyet Najat Al*-Ibad and *Risala fi Ijtima Al-Amr w Al-Nahi*. See: Al-Ameen, *A'yan Al-Shia*, 23:264; and Hirzeddine, *Ma'arif Al-Rijal*, 2:244.

[27] Hirzeddine, *Ma'arif Al-Rijal*, 2:235.

rise and sectarian hostility was spreading rapidly, even reaching Baghdad. It is said that the sedition and violence was caused by the Ottoman governor in Baghdad. The fact that he ignored addressing the grievances of the people and the scholars, along with his attempt to keep the Sultan uninformed, only made the situation worse.

Matters became even more difficult for Sayyid Al-Shirazi and the scholars in Samarra. The British ambassador tried to get involved in the situation and supposedly come to the Sayyid's aid. He traveled to Samarra to visit the Sayyid and offer his services to him. When he requested to meet with the Sayyid, the latter declined his overture. He refused to allow a foreigner the opportunity to meddle in the affairs of Muslims as he knew his purpose and motivations. The ambassador returned disappointed. The news of the sedition and violence finally reached the Sultan. He ordered that the fighting be immediately stopped and the flames of the violence were extinguished.

In India, the Marjaeya had yet another position that was illustrative of its engagement with British imperialism. There was a Shia charity in India that was endowed with sending financial support to scholars and poor families by way of the holy shrines.

The management and distribution of the money was under the supervision of the Marjaeya, such as Shaykh Al-Ansari during his time. However, when the British took rule over

India and heavily infiltrated both the public and private sectors, the Marjaeya took caution from the charity's money that could be seen as conceding to British imperial authority.

During that time period, the late Grand Ayatollah Shaykh Muhammad Taha Najaf was visited by a messenger of the organization. He wished to offer financial support from the organization to the Shaykh. The Shaykh recited the verses, "Say, 'O faithless ones! I do not worship what you worship.'"[28]

The messenger responded, "But I am a Muslim."

To that he replied, "Yes, but you are a tool for the faithless."[29]

For a long time that charity continued to be looked at with caution. My late grandfather Sayyid Al-Hakeem was even offered support from the organization before he became a Marja. Though he and his people were experiencing dire financial difficulties during that period, his integrity and self-respect would not allow him to accept the sum from that charity.[30]

When the English endeavored to spread their influence in Muslim nations they tried to gain the favor of the elites of Muslim society, which included the scholars, with money and

---

[28] The Holy Quran, 109:1-2.

[29] Hirzeddine, *Ma'arif Al-Rijal*, 2:108.

[30] Another great scholar that also refused to accept financial support from the charity in India under British imperial rule was Sayyid Hussain Al-Sayyid Ridha Bahreluloom (1221 – 1306 AH). He turned down huge sums of money coming from the organization, particularly an offer for him to receive 5000 English Rupees on a monthly basis. The Sayyid actually decided to move from Najaf to Karbala in order to avoid the situation altogether. See: Al-Ameen, *A'yan Al-Shia*, 26:58; and Al-Khaqani, *Shu'ara Al-Ghari*, 3:216.

gifts. They were mostly successful in this regard, which allowed them to build bridges for themselves in those societies and tactfully position themselves to have an impact on discourse and decision-making. The English tried this with the Marjaeya and the Shia scholars, but they failed miserably.

Take the example of Sir Ronald Storrs.[31] He, and those before him, failed in convincing the late Grand Ayatollah Sayyid Muhammad Kadhim Al-Tabatabaei Al-Yazdi to accept British gifts and overtures three consecutive times. They tried to appeal to the Sayyid by arguing that they wished for him to accept these gifts as financial support to be provided for the poor and needy. Storrs realized how different the Sayyid was, given his emphasis on honor and dignity over money and wealth. Storrs said, "Such a stance is the farthest from what is seen in Egypt and Hijaz in what are very similar circumstances."[32]

Storrs took a long look at the Sayyid. He recognized the secret behind this great man's eminence and influence. There was an unwavering strength illuminating from his tired grey eyes. Storrs felt the overwhelming prestige of his presence and the compelling attentiveness to his soft-spoken speech. In all of his experience with Muslim leaders and scholars

---

[31] Sir Ronald Henry Amherst Storrs was an official in the British Foreign and Colonial Office. He was known to speak the Arabic language fluently. While in Iraq, he visited the Holy City of Najaf where he met with politicians, scholars and other elites of Iraqi society.

[32] Al-Khalili, *Mawsoo'et Al-'Atabat Al-Muqadassa*, 1:257.

across Muslim nations, he realized there was none like this man.[33]

These sorts of stances and positions are not strange to us; in fact, we expect this of every religious man and woman, let alone our great scholars. Our example has been set for us by the Imams (a) and continues to be manifested through the leadership of the Marjaeya and the Islamic seminaries. The Marjaeya and the Seminary are a continuation of the school of the Imams (a). They set the illustrative example after them for the believers. If it were not for this responsibility and guidance, they would have been like other players of power and influence regardless of their religious stature.

The effect of all this was clear in the position Britain took in Iraq. The British chose not to work or engage with the Shia; rather, they ignored them and distressed them. They knew that the Shia formed a majority of what was oppressed under Ottoman rule – a regime that was staunchly anti-British.

Our scholars and Maraje took strong positions against the governments of their time when those institutions pushed policies that opposed Islamic values and principles. The scholars stood in the face of those regimes and would not concede to such policies, many of which were imported from foreign bodies, as they posed a threat to the fabric of Muslim society. The practice of faith was weakened because of the irresponsible and undignified actions of these governments.

---

[33] Ibid 1:256

The scholars condemned these policies just as they condemned the other transgressions of government and other apparent displays of corruption.

With the positions taken by the scholars, matters would sometimes escalate even further and the reactions intensified in their regard. Perhaps one of the most tragic examples of this came during the Pahlavi rule in Iran. Shah Rida Pahlavi wished to alter the nature of Iranian society. He wanted to transform it from piety and faith to worldliness and materialism. He was determined to do this by force. The religious scholars defiantly stood up against his will to corrupt their society. In return, they were met with forceful crackdowns that resulted in scores of executions, incarcerations, and exiles. The crackdowns were essentially a campaign to end the religious presence that so strongly existed in Iran. The Islamic Seminary of Qum was the safe haven that protected the religious scholars and survived the regime's vicious campaign. The scholars gathered in Qum under the guidance and leadership of the late Grand Ayatollah Shaykh Abdelkareem Al-Yazdi.

Even after that terrible period, the scholars would continue to face immense challenges. At the time, the late Grand Ayatollah Sayyid Al-Burujurdi[34] led the Islamic Seminary in Qum.

---

[34] Grand Ayatollah Sayyid Hussain Al-Sayyid Ali Al-Burujurdi (1292 – 1380 AH) was the religious authority and leader of the Islamic Seminary of Qum during his time. He cared deeply for strengthening ties between the different Islamic schools of thought and worked tirelessly to realize that. He has numerous publications in jurisprudence, the principles of jurisprudence, and the science of tradition and narrators. See: Al-Tehrani, *Nuqaba' Al-Bashar*, 1:609; and Al-Ansari, *Al-Mawsoo'a Al-Fiqhiyya Al-Muyassara*, 1:570.

The regime in Iran tried to pass legislation that was immoral and contradictory to Islamic principles. To that, Sayyid Al-Burujurdi made a decree against the government's actions. Acknowledging his influence with the people, the regime did not dare to pursue those goals. After he passed away, the cycle of corrupt government policies continued. With that, events would continue to transpire and what is known thereafter is indeed well-known.

In Iraq, our grandfather, Grand Ayatollah Sayyid Al-Hakeem was in a constant struggle with government and its legislation and policies that were at odds with Islamic principles. He held strong to his positions regarding the rule of the monarchy and about the regimes of Abd Al-Karim Qasim and Abdul Salam Arif. Because of the nature of their policies, the relationship between the late Sayyid and the government was very tense. At times the regime would seek him out and acede to his demands, and at other times it would not. It depended on the circumstances and the sort of interests involved. This inconsistency in principle and value was his test with them and would remain a grievance of his until his last days.

These principled stances of the religious scholars and the Marjaeya essentially made them a grave burden on the governments in their nations, as well as the foreign powers that backed those governments. The scholars were always in their calculations. Due to the burden and the threat they posed, these governments wished to eliminate scholars or at least silence them. This intent has been clear for a long time indeed and is characteristic of those who wish to infiltrate and rule over others. The struggle remains.

THE ROLE OF THE MARJAEYA

IS THE ROLE OF THE MARJAEYA TO SIMPLY GIVE EDICTS?

Is the role of the Marjaeya reduced to issuing edicts in jurisprudential matters and judging on cases and disputes between parties? Or does it encompass more than that in protecting the name of Islam, the general affairs of Muslims, and leading the faith and its people toward a better future? If this is part of the Marjaeya's job, then do you see it that more qualifications should be required for the Marja given what is needed in this day and age?

The primary job of a Muslim is to work in accordance to the religious rulings and etiquettes established by Islamic law. The intellect dictates this to be so, in order for one to relieve himself of liability before God – Who legislated those same rulings and etiquettes – and thus to be deserving of reward and salvation from punishment. The verses of the Holy Quran and the texts of the noble traditions emphasize this, complimenting what the intellect has already concluded.

There is no doubt that religious obligations include protecting Islam and guiding the faith and the Muslims towards what is best. However, these duties are not just for the Marja, but they are for all people to uphold.

Now, the guidelines and principles of our work must be according to the Islamic laws, and the only way to know those for non-jurists will be through *taqleed*. With differences in opinion amongst the varying jurists, *taqleed* is done in accordance to the regulations set forth in the jurists' treatise on Islamic laws derived from the legal proofs and evidence.

To set any other standard would mean manipulating religious rulings – something which signifies carelessness towards the responsibility of fulfilling the mentioned religious obligations. It would be an attempt to act in a way that is not permissible by God and would not clear an individual's responsibility towards Him. Of course, after the jurist sets the framework of religious obligations for himself and for the people, he can then seek the assistance of experts in fulfilling these obligations. This topic is discussed in further detail elsewhere in this book.

AGAINST DEVIANT IDEOLOGICAL MOVEMENTS

The Islamic Seminary and the Marjaeya have been known for their diligence in standing against deviant ideological movements. Do you think that the Marjaeya has been successful in facing the threats of these movements thus far?

Success in this regard is relative and contingent on the circumstances of the time. One of the most significant reasons for the decline of corrupt ideological movements in Islam generally, and Shiism particularly, is the strength of the religion and the school of thought. The Shia faith is built on reason and authenticity that speak to the depths of an individual's heart and mind, pressing its followers to accept its call and fulfill its obligations.

History has seen some of the world's most popular religions rise and decline within societies. Many were taken over or tainted with new movements that used the name of their faith and directed their communities away from their original course. Islam stands out, such that in all of its experiences it remains strong, authentic, and undiluted wherever it is. The permanence of Islam is due to the resilience of Shiism, for it is Islam's beating heart and its intellect. Shiism is the source of Islam's pure thought – free from delusions, superstitions, and contradictions. It is the voice of reason, truth and justice – the voice against tyranny, oppression, and injustice.

It is for this reason that you find anti-Islamic groups cozying up with fringe elements of the Muslim community. Their relationships develop as a result of common interests in diluting the faith or even destroying it altogether.

These ideological threats highlight the significance of the role of the Islamic seminaries in being the vanguard of intellectual thought and discourse in society, and protecting the pure and unified message of Shiism – especially during the long period of occultation in which our immaculate leaders are not directly leading their followers. During this period, everyone is free to express as they please, as it is the nature of religion – its teachings of creed and conduct – to be subjected to argumentations, misrepresentations and attempts at distortions and alterations from within. Add to that the external ideological movements as well as the designs and pressures from outside powers. The seminaries assume the responsibility of defending the faith against these threats and protecting the sanctity of Islamic thought and values. It has persevered against sedition and adversity, maintaining the principles of the faith and safeguarding it from adulteration. For over a thousand years it has done this, and will continue to do so with the help of God and the Imam (a).

Our recent history has witnessed the bitter discord between the *Usoolis* and *Akhbaris*, threatening the unity of the school of thought. Sedition did not prevail however. Individuals of wisdom and piety, from both sides, came together to settle the dispute, ease the tension, and focus on common principles instead. Unity was restored and extremism no longer had a place to be mentioned.

The school of thought then faced challenges with the *Shaykhis*, then the *Kashfis*, then the *Babis*, and finally the *Bahais*. Though these seditions of sorts followed one another, they did not pick up momentum and only declined. After some time, many returned to their faith and creed. They came back to the fold of Shiism and under the banner of Islam. Some of those who remained in those movements left Islam outright. Others stayed, but in their small groups detached from the body of Shiism, without having an impact or influence on the movement of the faith and its society.

This would not have happened without the inherent strength of Shiism and the work of the seminaries and their scholars. A quick comparison to other schools of thought can illustrate this further. Wahhabism began nearly two hundred years ago. Its movement intended to divide the Muslims further and disunite their voice. It played a huge role in weakening the Sunni caliphate of the time and ushering foreign influence into Muslim countries. Even up until the beginning of the twentieth century with the First World War, most Muslims looked at Wahhabism as a corrupt, foreign, and manufactured group that threatened the sanctity of Islam.

Gradually, however, with the decline of the Ottoman Empire, the voice of Sunnism quieted in this regard. Wahhabi activism increased and gained momentum in Sunni communities across the Muslim world. It is now the strongest, and the loudest group. It is seen to be the most apparent representative of Sunnism today. This is again due to its robust financial backing and the ongoing support that its movement receives. Sunnism was not strong enough to contain it theologically and ideologically, let alone defeat it.

Moreover, Islam was threatened by outside forces as well in the past century. The early strategies of colonialism – heavily based on the use of missionaries to win people's hearts as done in other parts of the world – utterly failed in Muslim countries. Their strategists realized that they could not convert Muslims to Christianity. Instead, they thought to strip Muslims away from Islam and their principles, by pushing them towards other pursuits. Along the way, people would belittle their faith, lean towards corruption, and justify their actions with slogans of alternative movements and calls to prosperity. This was promoted in the beginnings of colonialism in Muslim countries. No faith benefited from this, including Christianity, which was only exploited for the aims of those colonizing and subjugating other nations.

In the end, Muslims must realize the greatness of their religion and thank God for its blessings upon them. They should thank God for the blessing of being guided to this faith and sincerely hold on to it. For it was their faith that saved them, along with the leadership of the seminaries, making sure the exploited missionary campaigns would not succeed in their designs. Beyond those campaigns, the seminaries would go on to face and defeat the threat of communism and atheism decades later in the same way. Our great Maraje stood firm against these movements and made sure that the believers would remain honored and steadfast in their faith and creed.

The difference between the actions and effectiveness of the Marjaeya when compared to the other religious establishments of other schools and religions was clear. When the situation became tough, and the establishments of other schools were threatened, the seminaries were given the space to engage and have a greater presence. Take the example of Afghanistan. For quite a long time, the ruling authorities in Afghanistan placed a great deal of restrictions and suppressed the Shia generally, and their religious scholars more particularly. When communism took root in the country and began to spread, the authorities relaxed their restrictions on the Shia. The religious scholars and the seminaries there were able to be more active and speak more freely, as they stood against the spread of communism. The authorities acknowledged that the Shia were unique in their thought and education. They saw that they were able to connect to people both emotionally and intellectually. Given that, they realized that they were effective in spreading awareness against communism in ways that other religious groups were not.

Time and time again, Shiism proved its effectiveness and its diligence in standing for the truth and justice. Authorities learned that the Shia are a power to acknowledge and reckon with.

We ask God Almighty to strengthen the faith and support it, to support the religious seminaries to continue on the straight path, to guide the believers to turn back to the seminaries and support them in standing against deviant ideologies and protect the tenets and teachings of Shiism. All this would be a fulfillment of the words of the Holy Prophet (s), "There will always be a group from within my nation who support the truth and who will be unshaken by the abandonment of those who abandon it."[1] Their support of the truth is a projection of their true call, "So that he who perishes might perish by a manifest proof, and he who lives may live on by a manifest proof…"[2]

We seek refuge in God from sedition, deviance, ill outcomes, disgrace in this world, and chastisement in the hereafter – surely, He is the most merciful.

DETACHMENT FROM THE PEOPLE?

Some think that the Marja is detached from the people and the troubles they face. What is your take on this especially in your role as a Marja?

Islam has stressed that all Muslims must care for the issues that Muslims generally face. It has been narrated that if a Muslim wakes up in the morning and is not concerned with the state of his fellow Muslim, then he is not a Muslim at all.[3]

---

[1] Al-Bukhari, *Sahih Bukhari*, 4:178.
[2] The Holy Quran, 8:42.
[3] Al-Amili, *Wasai'l Al-Shia*, 11:18.

It is also narrated that a believer is to support his fellow believer like building blocks for a structure, they build on to one
another and hold each other up.[4]

Thus, caring for the affairs of Muslims is required of all Muslims, then what can be said of what is expected from the
scholars of the faith and the Marjaeya? These individuals have
a deeper understanding of the teachings and laws of Islam.
They also have great insight into the challenges facing the
community because of their deep involvement with the community. Caring for the affairs of the community is deeply
rooted in the role of the Marjaeya. Two particular things testify to this.

Firstly, it is too often that the Marja has to put aside his traditional studies and many of his private commitments because of his commitment with helping the community in its
problems and challenges. He does this because even though
he spent much of his life immersed in his studies and worship, he sees that helping and caring for the people is much
more important.

Secondly, the Marja frequently faces tests and trials from the
enemies of the nation. If it were not for his constant pursuit
for the betterment of the people's condition, defending their
honor and demanding their rights, he would not be faced
with such enmity. The Marja's deep concern and care for the
affairs of the people puts him at the forefront of the pressure
of external forces that want to harm the people.

---

[4] Al-Bukhari, *Sahih Al-Bukhari*, 1:123.

There are so many stances taken by our great Maraje against oppression and oppressors. They defended the rights of the weak and the oppressed. They worked to better their situations and lift them from being in need, both publicly and privately.

During the rule of the Qajar dynasty, the great Marja Shaykh Kashif Al-Ghita'[5] beseeched Sultan Fateh Ali Shah to release a group of Ottoman prisoners that were being held by the authorities.[6] He wished to ease the tension that was rising between the two states and deter further travesties between the two Muslim nations.

The Shaykh went on to fortify and defend the Holy City of Najaf from the violent raids of the Wahhabis that wished to destroy the city just as they did to Karbala. He rallied the scholars and community members of Najaf to pick up arms and defend the city. He led the mobilization to train the volunteers in weaponry and standing their ground against the oncoming attacks. The Shaykh, and the scholars, were one with the people. They stood their ground, firmly hand-in-hand, defending their city.[7] The details of these stances have been recorded by historians and relayed by the people, one generation to the next.

---

[5] Shaykh Ja'far Al-Shaykh Khodr Kashif Al-Ghataa' (1154 – 1227 AH) was the grand Marja of his time. He lived and passed in the Holy City of Najaf, and was widely known for his deep knowledge and wisdom. One of his notable works was *Sharh Qawa'id Al-Allamah Al-Hilli*.

[6] Hirzeddine, *Ma'arif Al-Rijal*, 1:151.

[7] Aal Mahboubah, *Maadi Al-Najaf w Hadhareha*, 3:137.

Shaykh Kashif Al-Ghita' played an instrumental role in protecting the people of Najaf from both internal strife and external injustice. He was a safe haven for the weak and oppressed. This role was especially seen during the sedition that took place between the two groups in Najaf: Al-Shimirt and Al-Zigirt.[8] Moreover, the Shaykh saved the people of Najaf from the many exorbitant taxes levied by the Ottomans.[9]

His son Shaykh Moussa[10], who became the Marja after him, prevented the Ottoman governor Dawoud Basha from instituting conscription for the people of Najaf.[11] Dawoud Basha admired him greatly and conceded to Shaykh Moussa.[12] Moreover, he played the instrumental role of mediating relations between the Iranian and Ottoman states, as well as curbing more conflict between their two peoples. Shaykh Moussa was noted for his wisdom and prudence with his foresight to protect the treasury of the Shrine of Imam Ali (a) from being sacked by the Wahhabis. He had its items duly recorded and transferred to Baghdad as a precaution against any possible attacks.

---

[8] Ibid, 3:138.

[9] Ibid, 3:138.

[10] Shaykh Moussa Al-Shaykh Ja'far Kashif Al-Ghataa' (1180 – 1243 AH) was a Marja in the Holy City of Najaf. He was widely known in Iraq and Iran as a peacemaker between Iran and Turkey. One of his notable works was *Ahkam Al-Salat*.

[11] Aal Mahboubah, *Maadi Al-Najaf w Hadhareha*, 3:201.

[12] Hirzeddine, *Ma'arif Al-Rijal*, 3:27.

His brother, Shaykh Hassan[13], was praised for preventing a grave attack on the Holy City of Najaf by the Ottoman governor Najeeb Basha. After attacking the Holy City of Karbala, his army moved towards Najaf with the intent to destroy it as well. Shaykh Hassan intercepted Najeeb Basha before his army began its attack. In his exchange with him, Shaykh Hassan was able to successfully dissuade the governor from pursuing the attack.[14] They entered the city peacefully without causing any harm. The Shaykh was well regarded for defending the rights of the Shia in numerous occasions, including situations in Baghdad during the rule of the very same governor. He also played an instrumental role in easing the tensions and keeping the peace between the Al-Shimirt and Al-Zigirt groups in Najaf.

Shaykh Sahib Al-Jawahir was another scholar known for his valiant stances of bravery. He was widely regarded for standing up for the people of Najaf when the city was hit with the plague in 1247 AH. He rushed towards assisting and aiding them with all that he could. The same was the stance of Sayyid Muhammad Baqir Al-Qazwini[15], who was at the forefront

---

[13] Shaykh Hassan Al-Shaykh Ja'far Kashif Al-Ghataa' (1180 – 1243 AH) was a great scholar and Marja of his time. He helped lead the effort in training and equipping the people of Najaf to defend their holy city from foreign attacks and raids. One of his most notable publications is *Anwar Al-Faqaha*.

[14] Hirzeddine, *Ma'arif Al-Rijal*, 1:213.

[15] Sayyid Muhammad Baqir Al-Sayyid Ahmad Al-Qazwini was one of the great jurists of the Holy City of Najaf. He organized people in the neighborhoods of Najaf during the plague. He prepared first-aid kits and treatment for the sick. In addition, he was responsible for overseeing the proper burial of approximately forty thousand persons that died from the plague in Najaf. He made sure that all of their families were cared for after they passed. After all of his work he would be one of the last people in the city to die of the plague.

of organizing and helping people during this awful time. Sayyid Al-Qazwini was also widely regarded for initiating a project of channeling drinking water to the Holy City of Najaf. The project was later completed by Sayyid Asadallah Al-Rashti.[16]

When the city of Najaf experienced unprecedented price hikes, Sayyid Al-Shirazi Al-Kabeer quickly moved to alleviate the harsh impact on the people. For every cluster of stores and neighborhoods in the city, he assigned a group of individuals to pass out grain to all those in need. He carried out this project until the next harvest came, prices went down, and people were relieved.[17] He would take it upon himself to collect clothing and foodstuffs for people living in rural areas, as well as the poor and destitute, twice a year.[18]

When Sayyid Al-Shirazi went to Samarra he had a bridge built for those who lived near the Tigris River. The project had cost about one thousand Ottoman Liras. It made it much easier for the residents and visitors to travel in the area and helped provide for some vital services in Samarra.[19]

The late Shaykh Muhammad Al-Sherbayani[20] would go on to witness the hardship of many pilgrims that traveled by foot

---

[16] Hirzeddine, *Ma'arif Al-Rijal*, 2:228.

[17] Al-Wardi, *Lamahat Ijtima'iya min Tarikh Al-Iraq Al-Hadeeth*, 3:88.

[18] Hirzeddine, *Ma'arif Al-Rijal*, 2:235.

[19] Al-Wardi, *Lamahat Ijtima'iya min Tarikh Al-Iraq Al-Hadeeth*, 3:9.

[20] Shaykh Muhammad ibn Al-Mawla Mufadhal Ali Al-Sherbayani (1245 – 1322 AH) was one of the Maraje of the Holy City of Najaf. He was known for his special care for orphans, widows, and visitors of the Holy City. He was regarded for establishing a school for students of the seminary. When the Shaykh passed

from Najaf to Mecca for hajj. The path they took through Mount Hayel was indeed a dangerous one. Wishing to protect the pilgrims from peril, he forbade his followers from taking that route. The other contemporary scholars agreed with his move and did the same. Thus, the road was cut off for a few years.[21] The Iranian government was forced to make that travel route unlawful and provide an alternative course.

And when the visitors of Imam Hussain (a) would pass through Najaf on their way to Karbala, the late Marja Shaykh Muhammad Taha would host them in a large inn for them to sleep and rest. It was important to him that the visitors were taken care of.

The past two centuries have seen so many examples of our scholars making it their top priority to serve people and ensure their wellbeing.

During the last days of Ottoman involvement in Iraq, the Ottomans had attacked the Holy City of Najaf. Mortars hit the Shrine of Imam Ali (a) and a number of people were hurt. The late Marja Sayyid Muhammad Kadhim Al-Yazdi immediately sent word to the Ottoman capital condemning the blatant transgression against innocent people and the sanctity of the Shrine.[22]

The same Sayyid Al-Yazdi would also establish a large inn in the Holy City of Najaf for the visitors of the shrines. The inn

---

away he did not own a home, or any property for that matter, as he put any money he had towards projects for the community.

[21] Hirzeddine, *Ma'arif Al-Rijal*, 2:373.

[22] Al-Khalili, *Mawsoo'at Al-'Atabat Al-Muqaddasa*, 1:251.

stayed open and in use until only years ago. His sons went back to our grandfather Sayyid Al-Hakeem regarding the use of the inn. He decided to turn it into a religious school and spent large sums of money for the establishment; however, it was eventually destroyed in the course of fighting.

During the same era, the late Marja Sayyid Abulhassan Al-Asfahani suggested to the governor of the time, during a meeting with him, that he build a bridge on the Tigris River to make travel easier for the visitors to Samarra. The bridge that the late Sayyid Al-Shirazi had built years prior to that had deteriorated. Though traveling in that area was restricted to the riverside, his request was not fulfilled. Still, he continued to make it his priority to do what he could to ease the pain and hardship of people. As a result of the Second World War, Najaf experienced a wheat crisis in which many people suffered. Sayyid Al-Asfahani took it upon himself to make sure all were fed in the city. He ordered that more bakeries be opened and recreation be increased in the community. The hardship of wartime actually turned into a time of blessing and bestowal upon the poor and needy.[23]

The late Shaykh Muhammad Hussain Kashif Al-Ghita', along with a group of scholars, would later demand for Shia rights in Iraq during the reign of the new monarchy. He was able to garner the support of many; however, those who would rise in protest with him later abandoned him. Thus, he was not

---

[23] *Majallat Al-Daleel*, Issue: 3.4, 135.

able to achieve what he set out to do for them and the people inevitably suffered more abuses by the state.

The tenure of our grandfather the late Sayyid Al-Hakeem was known for its focus on the believers both in and outside of Iraq. He made it a priority to solve community problems, demand for people's rights, and lift them up from oppression. He cared deeply for the issues they faced and spent much time on religious education. Unifying people and bringing them closer together was very important to him. Muslim communities across the world are thankful and appreciative for the work he did to this very day. Those that came after him would continue what they could with the dire circumstances and challenges they faced. They would carry on with patience and wisdom, as they had no one but God to rely on.

This account of the work of the Maraje in Iraq is only a glimpse into history from the past couple of centuries. There is much more that took place outside of this specific timeframe, as well as the experiences of Maraje outside of Iraq – especially in Iran where the capabilities and opportunities to the Marjaeya were greater. We won't delve into that history due to the brief nature of this work.

Throughout history, the Marjaeya has been known for its commitment to utilizing portions of the religious dues afforded to them to establish beneficial projects for the community – such as mosques, community centers, shelters, and housing. It has also spent greatly on projects dedicated to helping the poor and needy. This is something that cannot be ignored or taken for granted. Even though there have been differences in implementation as a result of differing opinions and capabilities between Maraje, there has always been a great emphasis in this regard.

Moreover, the Marjaeya has always worked tirelessly on education. They realized the significance of education in building the character of a nation and advancing it forward. It would be apt for us to briefly show the efforts exerted in this regard, even if the results desired have not always been realized due to unexpected circumstances or preventions internally or externally. What is most important is the actual pursuit and striving for what is best for the nation. The results are in the hands of God.

In the beginning of the last Hijri century, our scholars saw the dire need for educated youth given the stagnation in culture and education in Iraq during the latter part of Ottoman rule. The Marjaeya, and the seminary generally, sought to address this need by establishing religious schools known as *Al-Madaris Al-Ja'feria*. With the permission of the Marjaeya, religious dues were spent on the establishment and growth of these educational institutions. The religious scholars significantly backed these schools and supported them in various ways, especially with their time and presence.

The great scholar Sayyid Muhammad Saeed Al-Haboubi used to attend the functions and events of the schools, showing a great deal of support and encouragement for its programs and establishment. In some occasions, certain events were followed by celebrations outside with fireworks filling the night sky. The faces of the families would in turn be filled with cheer and joy. The Sayyid too was cheerful, and especially hopeful in all the good that would come from that establishment.

The late Marja Sayyid Abulhassan Al-Asfahani and the late Marja Shaykh Muhammad Ridha Yaseen would go on to establish *Jam'iyyat Muntada Al-Nashr*[24] – a publishing house. It was tasked with launching a college for religious studies and opening schools in a number of cities across Iraq like Najaf and Kadhimiya.[25] The purpose of all of this was to raise a generation of religious youth that would carry out its responsibility in serving its community. These projects encouraged other members of society with greater means to open up more schools as well. The late Balasim Al-Yaseen was one of those individuals – he established a school under his care in his neighborhood. Similarly, other representatives of the Maraje would open up schools in their localities.

---

[24] Jam'iyyat Muntada Al-Nashr was established in the Holy City of Najaf in 1935. It formed based on the idea of adjusting and advancing the current curriculum to the consider the needs of the religious scholar of the time. Its members published a number of books exemplifying the institution's purpose such as *Al-Mantiq*, *Usool Al-Fiqh*, *and 'Aqaid Al-Imamiya* by Shaykh Muhammad Ridah Al-Muthaffar, as well as Al-*Usool Al-Aamma lil-Fiqh Al-Muqarin* and *Al-Qawa'id Al-Aamma fil-Fiqh Al-Muqarin* by Sayyid Muhammad Taqi Al-Hakeem and *Muhadharat fi Al-Tareekh Al-Islami* by Shaykh Muhammad Mahdi Chamseddine. A committee dedicated for sermons and lectures was established in 1364 AH for the purpose of guiding the young lecturers and providing the proper ways of delivering messages on the pulpit. Other colleges, along with publications by each of those colleges, were established such as the Fiqh College and its publication *Al-Najaf*.

[25] These schools ranged from elementary to high school. They were established with two goals: advancing religious education and excelling in traditional public education. Both the schools and the colleges established by the Jam'iyya graduated hundreds of students in religious studies. Many of Iraq's writers, teachers, activists, poets, and lecturers were graduates of these institutions.

Some scholars would go on to establish *Al-Mujamma' Al-Thaqafi*[26] at Muntada Al-Nashr. The project was very active and held weekly functions of research and discourse. It printed its research and findings in a number of publications and books produced by the publishing house itself.

Our grandfather cared deeply for these projects. When the general manager of religious endowments in Iraq, Abdulrahman Khidr, visited our grandfather in his home he expressed his concern for the problem of religious education in Iraq. The late Sayyid told him that religious education was being gravely neglected in public schools. The general manager assured him that he would take care of it. He promised him that he would see to it that the Shia areas of Iraq will have a Shia curriculum.

However, his bigotry blinded him and he did not fulfill any of his promises. That truly upset the late Sayyid, so much so that the next time the general manager came to visit him he was told that the Sayyid did not wish to see him. He left frustrated. Nonetheless, the late Sayyid remained diligent in his effort to find opportunities to support the advancement of education. He supported the establishment of *Madaris Al-*

---

[26] Al-Mujamma' Al-Thaqafi at Muntada Al-Nashr was one of the projects of the publishing house. It launched with a grand celebration in 1956 on the occasion of the Holy Prophet's (s) and Imam Al-Sadiq's (a) birthday. The project took it upon itself to revive the tradition of celebrating religious holidays and holding educational and cultural functions that would showcase Shia thought.

Imam Al-Jawad[27] as well as the Usool Al-Deen College[28] in Baghdad. Both establishments were under his supervision and support.

The late Sayyid was very keen on engagement in education. Thus, he sent the esteemed researcher Ayatollah Sayyid Muhammad Taqi Al-Hakeem[29] to be a lecturer at the University of Baghdad. Our grandfather endeavored to establish and expand the University of Kufa; however, the circumstances of the time prevented that project from being realized during his lifetime.

Moreover, he emphasized that the scholars of the seminary participate in conferences that took place outside of Iraq. He supported such projects greatly and sent a number of representatives on his behalf to some of these regional and international conferences. The purpose was to let the world hear

---

[27] Madaris Al-Imam Al-Jawad or Al-Jawad Schools focused on creating study programs that combined both religious and secular studies, in accordance to curriculum standards of the ministry of education. Its schools were opened in Kathimiya, Basra, and other cities across Iraq.

[28] Usool Al-Deen College was established in 1964 in Baghdad, Iraq. Its programs were organized on the idea of bringing together religious studies and secular studies. After the passing the late Sayyid Al-Hakeem it was transformed into a night school and later on merged with the College of Arts at the University of Baghdad.

[29] Ayatollah Sayyid Muhammad Taqi Al-Hakeem (1924 – 2002) was from the great jurists of the Islamic Seminary in the Holy City of Najaf. He worked closely with Shaykh Muhammad Ridha Al-Muthaffar and other high scholars in administrating Jam'iyyat Muntada Al-Nashr. He was the head of the Fiqh College and led many research projects for advanced research at the University of Baghdad. He was selected to serve on the boards of Al-Mujamma' Al-Ilmi Al-Iraqi in 1964, Mujamma' Al-Lugha Al-Arabiyya in Cairo, Egypt in 1967, Mujamma' Al-Lugha Al-Arabiyya in Damascus, Syria in 1972, Mujamma' Al-Lugha Al-Arabiyya in Amman, Jordan in 1980 and Mujamma' Al-Hadhara Al-Islamiyya Al-Urduniyya in 1981. Some of his most notable works were *Al-Usool Al-Aamma lil-Fiqh Al-Muqarin*, *Al-Qawa'id Al-Aamma fil-Fiqh Al-Muqarin, and Al-Tashayyu' fi Nadawat Al-Qahira (Shiism in the Forums of Cairo).*

the voice of Shiism and communicate its proper message to people, both near and far.

The Marjaeya also promoted making education more accessible through establishing public libraries. The late Sayyid made it a priority to establish his grand library open for the public.[30] It became a go-to place for researchers and writers, as it gathered some of the most important resources both contemporary and historic. He went on to open a number of branches to the library so more people can have access and benefit from it. A total of sixty-six branches were opened inside and outside of Iraq, one of which was in Al-Azhar University in Cairo, Egypt. These libraries had a tremendous impact on spreading the teachings of our faith and educating the Islamic world about Shiism.

The late Marja Ayatollah Sayyid Muhsen Al-Ameen[31] would go on to establish a number of schools for the Shia community in Syria. He gave special attention to education and more particularly religious education based on the teachings of the school of thought. The late Ayatollah Sayyid Abdulhussain

---

[30] The Imam Al-Hakeem Public Library opened its doors in 1966. It was one of the most advanced and resourceful libraries of the time. Its branches spread to numerous countries such as Indonesia, Syria, Iran, Lebanon, Egypt, India, and Pakistan.

[31] Ayatollah Sayyid Muhsen Al-Sayyid Abdelkarim Al-Ameen (1282 – 1371 AH) was born in the village of Shaqra in the Jabal Amel region of Lebanon. He studied in the Holy City of Najaf until he reached the level of ijtihad. He traveled to Syria to settle in Damascus in 1319 AH. He was very focused on writing, lecturing, and education and cared deeply for the affairs of society, religion, and the nation. The late Sayyid Al-Ameen established schools for boys and girls to combine religious and secular studies to ensure students had a wholesome and comprehensive education. He was an esteemed historian, a poet, and a man of letters. Some of his most notable publications include *A'yan Al-Shia, Al-Dur Al-Thameen, and Al-Raheeq Al-Makhtoom*.

Sharafeddine, who was a renowned researcher and jurist, cared deeply for these issues as well. He established the Ja'fari College in Tyre, Lebanon for the purpose of educating the youth of *Jabal Amel*[32]. He also established a school for females, acknowledging the importance of girls' education and providing an alternative to the western school systems that did not give consideration to religious teachings and guidance.

There is much more that can be discussed of the work of our scholars in different places across the region, under the care of the Marjaeya. This can be especially said of Iran where the capabilities and opportunities for projects were much greater. Again, we won't delve into that due to the brief nature of this work and hope we did not do injustice to those that we neglected to mention here.

The Marjaeya also established many educational foundations in western countries that have significant Muslim populations. The effort to support these organizations and their projects are ongoing due to the great need for them in their communities. Without organizations and projects that educate the youth in the West, those communities would be at risk of becoming lost. Instead of the youth being ambassadors of Islam and the faith through knowing its true teachings and ethics, we may lose them altogether. It is upon every responsible Muslim to have a sense of duty towards projects that provide education and awareness to our youth. "As for

---

[32] Jabal Amel is a mountainous region in South Lebanon. It is known to be one of the earliest communities of Shia Muslims in Islamic history. – Eds.

those who strive in Us, We shall surely guide them in Our ways, and God is indeed with the virtuous."[33]

In addition to all of this, the Marjaeya has always placed a great deal of emphasis on writing and publishing books across diverse disciplines for the benefit of the community's education and preserving its heritage. The Marjaeya and the seminary have continued to make this, along with all the other education-based projects for the benefit of the community, a top priority.

So when did the Shia Maraje ever rest at ease or seem unconcerned? Did their trials ever end? Did they ever rest their aspirations? All out of concern for the trials and troubles that faced the religion and the believers.

God alone knows their state and rewards their deeds. Indeed, He shall suffice us and He is the best of guardians.

THE REALITIES WE FACE

There are certainly some realities that we face that should be discussed and clarified.

For one, the capabilities of the Marjaeya are limited. The Marjaeya does not hold any official political authority, for religious and ethical reasons, as it refuses to compromise its autonomy with any recognized government or power. It does not hold any power more than the trust that the believers

---

[33] The Holy Quran, 29:69.

place in it. Too often it cannot impose itself against the powers that surround it. Rather, it finds itself surrounded by such powers from every aspect, just as suppressed nations are surrounded by oppressors. With the plurality of Maraje it only adds complexity to an already complicated situation – especially given the reality of differing views and outlooks between the jurists in many circumstances.

Secondly, the Marjaeya has a great responsibility that consumes most of its time and resources – that is developing and maintaining the Islamic seminary. The seminary is the focal point of Islamic teachings and its dissemination. The faith is spread and its voice is heard through the hard working scholars that the seminary produces. They spend their lives learning and educating the people about the faith and their teachings. For this responsibility, there are priorities:

1) Giving the seminary its due significance, for without it the symbols of the faith as well as its teachings would be lost.

2) The Marjaeya is the sole body that can take the lead role in safeguarding and maintaining the seminary. The other forces of good, existent in the believing community, are not capable of fulfilling this responsibility without the Marjaeya. The Marjaeya has maintained the seminaries with due diligence. Still, the good seminary student remains tired and fatigued in most cases.

3) The Marjaeya refuses to go out and seek assistance for the services of the seminary, nor does it market

or advertise its functions and activities. Many of the programs and services that they arrange are unknown to the public, except those who directly receive the benefit of those services. This is due to the Marjaeya's natural tendency to not wish for its work to be marketed. Its priority is to carry out its duties, with a clear conscience, and serve the people in the way of God. For that, it often stresses anonymity when it comes to the services it provides. Its work is for God, not publicity.

Some of those who worked with my grandfather, the late Sayyid Al-Hakeem, argued that they should publicize and market some of the services they provide to highlight the importance of the Marjaeya and its presence. My grandfather was not convinced. It was more important to him that the work was done with sincerity and pure intentions. In the end, each person is entitled to his opinion and each is rewarded based on his intention.

In any case, the third priority listed above was a reason for much of the work and services of the seminary going unnoticed. Perhaps much of the work was recorded within the texts of different individual books; but, that would require much time and effort to look through, a luxury not afforded to most. Moreover, the first two priorities relatively contributed to fewer activities and functions as well. This, however, does not mean that the history of the Marjaeya and its noble work has completely gone unnoticed.

We still feel what many of the believers that live alongside and experience the seminaries and the Marjaeya hold feelings of pride, honor, respect, and appreciation to the Marjaeya and the scholars. The believers look at the Marjaeya as a loving and gracious father – he is saddened by their sorrow, delighted by their joy, and is there for them through their trials and hardship.

Nonetheless, it is indeed peculiar to hear some of these questions about the Marjaeya. As it seems people have forgotten history and are too quick to mischaracterize and judge situations without contemplation. It was only years ago that the Iranian Revolution took place. That revolution validated itself by being under the care of the Marjaeya, which proved its solidarity, perseverance, and sincerity throughout history in a way that cannot be compared. After the revolution, all the seminaries were exposed to further hardship especially in places like Afghanistan and Pakistan. It would be expected that the believing youth would feel the pain of the Marjaeya and the seminaries that their hearts would be broken for the oppression their scholars would endure. Instead, the Marjaeya was faced with this current phenomena of shocking doubts and suspicions – ones that ignore the deep struggles, stances, and sacrifices made by the Marjaeya and the seminaries. What has happened? Why is reality so easily ignored? Why are truths so easily forgotten? But the longer you live, the more wonders you see!

This subject truly breaks my heart. It is not for the oppression of truth and the insistence on ignoring reality – that is something that we have experienced throughout our history. Nor is it that such oppression to the truth comes from our sons, even though being oppressed by your close ones is much more devastating than being oppressed by strangers. Rather, it is for the following two reasons.

Firstly, these attitudes transgress on the sanctity of the Marjaeya, which is a transgression against the sanctity of the Awaited Imam (aj). For he did not leave his followers until he ordered them to revert to their scholars in his absence. Through them the faith is protected and the proof upon the people is established. Imam Al-Sadiq (a) said, "Know the position of men with us based on their ability to narrate from us."[34] Imam Al-Hadi (a) would go on to say years later, "Be steadfast in your religion, for whoever grows old in our love and strives in our cause, will be sufficed by the will of God."[35]

Finally, the Awaited Imam Al-Mahdi (aj) said, "In regards to the contemporary matters, refer to the narrators of our tradition. For they are my proof upon you, and I am the proof of God."[36]

Did the Imam (a) refer the Shia to the scholars when there wasn't in every generation those who are qualified and sincere to be entrusted with this responsibility? God forbid that that would be the case! There is no doubt that he knew that in

---

[34] Al-Amili, *Wasai'l Al-Shia*, 18:109.

[35] Ibid, 18:110.

[36] Ibid, 18:101.

every age there would be individuals who would be qualified for the position and trustworthy with such responsibility. Studying the history of the scholars from the times of the Imams (a) to our day and age shows that they certainly met these expectations. To have this suspicious attitude towards the Marjaeya would be to deny this very truth and belittle the guidance by our Awaited Imam (aj).

Second, we are worried for our sons. Our Imams (a) promised us that during the time of occultation many will depart from the faith. Al-Mufaddal ibn Umar narrates from Imam Al-Sadiq (a),

> *By God, your Imam will disappear for years during your time. You will be tested until it is questioned, "Did he die? Was he killed? Did he perish? Which valley did he pursue?" The eyes of the believers will cry for him. And you will be thrashed just as the waves of the sea thrash against sailing ships. None will be saved except he who God has taken an oath from [and he has fulfilled that oath], and faith was written in his heart, and is supported by His spirit.*

Al-Mufaddal cried and then asked, "How will we [go on]?" The Imam (a) then peered outside towards the sun and asked him, "Do you see the sun?" Al-Mufaddal looked out and said, "Yes." The Imam (a) then said, "By God, our matter is more apparent than this sun."[37]

Ali ibn Ja'far narrates from his brother Imam Moussa Al-Kadhim (a), "If the Fifth from the progeny of the Seventh

---

[37] Al-Kulayni, *Al-Kafi*, 1:336.

disappears, then beseech God in your faith… My son, there is no doubt that the Master of this matter [the Imamate] will [enter] occultation so that those who claim belief in this matter will stop believing. It is a trial from God, with which He has tested His creation…"[38]

Hassan ibn Mahboob narrates from Imam Al-Rida (a), "There must be a dark sedition where every advisor and guardian will fall by the wayside, and that is with the Shia's loss of the Third from my progeny…"[39]

These narrations promise that the believers will be exposed to blind seditions and the dark storms of deviation, which will complicate matters for them and make them heedless of the cause of the Household (a). And though their cause is clearer than the sun itself, people will leave the faith and in that is eternal devastation and suffering.

The greatest barrier to such deviation is the presence of the seminaries and the Marjaeya, because they make it their duty to expose falsities and clarify truths. By this, the religion is protected and the cause of the Household (a) is safeguarded throughout this long occultation.

If this campaign of deviance were to be successful in stripping the believers away from the Marjaeya and the seminaries through shaking their trust in them, the believers would be at a grave loss, as they will be critically vulnerable to swaying from their faith and being toyed with by others.

---

[38] Al-Kulayni, *Al-Kafi*, 1:336.

[39] Al-Sadouq, *Kamal Al-Deen*, 335.

We warn the believers to safeguard themselves and their faith from this grave danger. Surely, faith is the guardian of your matters and the cause of your joy, salvation, and victory. Do not let go of it.

Soon, this trend may become part of the plans of the forces of evil to misguide the believers. They will make use of the rising voices of skepticism, renunciation, and indifference toward the tenets and teachings of the sect. They will employ people's audacity to ignore clear truths, attempts to abandon the path of the Holy Household, and the rising wave of materialism and deviance.

A LOOK INTO THE FUTURE

AN OUTLOOK OF HOPE OR WORRY

> *As a religious authority and a leader in the Islamic world, is your outlook of the future one of hope or worry?*

There is no doubt that the troubles we have are many and the problems we face are indeed complex. However, Shiism has endured numerous crises throughout the centuries and remained standing after it all, with the help of God and the guidance of the Ahlulbayt (a). Its teachings were crystalized, its presence was fortified, and it became a reality that others had no choice but to acknowledge and reckon with.

For Shiism, whose seed the Holy Prophet (s) planted and watered, was faced with a grave calamity after the death of the Prophet (s), which threatened its existence. Its opposition was able to grab the reins of power and ascend to the helm. They made it a priority to entrench their opposing existence, fortify their authority, and silence those who spoke out against them, or even eradicate them.

Still, there was a small group of believers that remained loyal to the seed the Prophet (s) planted and held on to the creed and its principles. They were able, with their wisdom and patience, to protect that seed and nurture its growth until it could one day produce its fruit. It was through the unmatched leadership of the Commander of the Faithful (a) that Shiism survived, and would ultimately be embodied in his person. The movement continued steadily and quietly with reason and pragmatism, so that more and more Muslims would come to understand it and pursue it. From then on, its supporters only grew in number.

Through the person of the Commander of the Faithful (a), the movement was victorious. It was able to take the caliphate and the helm from amongst all the different opposition groups that stood against the third caliph Uthman. Imam Ali (a) revived Shiism once more through this role that he played, outwardly expressing and establishing its teachings for the people even throughout all the struggles that endured during his caliphate. When he was assassinated and the Umayyads rose to power, the thought was that Shiism had ended.

The Umayyads presumed that by killing off the leader of the movement, it would inevitably kill the movement itself. They did not know the extent of loyalty and allegiance entrenched in the hearts and souls of his followers. In fact, Muawiya was bewildered by their unwavering allegiance to Imam Ali (a). He would say that he was more baffled by their love for him after his death more so than their support for him while he was alive. For that, Muawiya made it a top priority to battle Shiism by all the means at his disposal, employing the most vicious tactics of defamation, suppression, and violence against the Shia. With all the harm he caused and all his efforts to defame Shiism, he still failed.

Muawiya died and his son Yazid would continue his father's work. The Shia mobilized in opposition to the new Umayyad caliphate, which ended in the tragedy of Karbala – the massacre of Imam Hussain (a) and his companions, who were individuals willing to sacrifice for their principles.

The existence of Shiism was once again threatened in such tragic circumstances. It was, in the view of its enemies as well as many of its own supporters, seen as a political movement that ended with the death of its leader Imam Hussain (a). The view was that this movement was quelled like the many other opposition groups. Take the examples of the revolution of Medina that was suppressed with brutal bloodshed, and the movement of Ibn Zubayr in Mecca that also ended with his death and the defiling of the Kaaba.

However, the believers – though few in number – remained firm in their creed and principles. They were able by their solidarity, patience, the guidance of the Imams (a) and the protection of God to project themselves into the reality of Islam. By the time Shiism's teachings were crystalized once again within the public and its movement gained new momentum, it faced further oppression and subjugation. It reached its peak with the martyrdom of Imam Al-Kadhim (a).

He was so oppressed that even his sacred body was mistreated. His enemies carried so much hate within them, further illustrating the reality of their own creed and belief. One of oppressors would wretchedly call out, in reference to Imam Al-Kadhim (a), "This is the leader of the Rejectionists!"[1]

Compare that with the internal divide that took place within Shiism from the Al-Waqifa movement after his death as well. It threatened to vehemently shake the foundations of Shiism, if it were not for the solidarity of those who had foresight and the leadership of Imam Al-Rida (a). The people gave allegiance to him and through him there was victory. The ruling authority found itself, once again, with no choice but to recognize and reckon with the Shia – even if there was resistance and violence at times.

Then came the great test with the occultation of Imam Al-Mahdi (a). The Shia would be devastated with the loss of their guardian and what followed of division and disunity between groups and their creed. People would have thought this to cause the disorientation of the teachings of Shiism, let alone the demise of the faith in its entirety. But the Shia only persevered and would be strengthened in their faith and resolve. Their creed matured and crystalized, their scholars delved further in knowledge and wisdom, the believers grew stronger in their foundations, and Shiism proved that it could withstand the hardships of reality – even with the absence of

---

[1] Al-Sadouq, *'Uyoun Akhbar Al-Rida*, 1:99.

their Imam. It is just as our Imams (a) said, that God would not have had Imam Al-Mahdi (aj) go into occultation unless He knew that there would be believers who would be steadfast in such a trying time.[2]

Tests, trials, tribulation, and hardship only increase in number and intensity during the occultation. At the same time, the manifest proof of Shiism becomes more apparent and its voice only gets stronger. Today, it speaks in the name of the true Islam as it opposes oppression, disbelief, and injustice.

It is only natural that the forces of oppression and evil today would be allies of one another against Shiism. Through inciting internal disputes and sedition, as well as attacking it from the outside by brute force, they have made Shiism a target. Murder, imprisonment, depravation, and displacement are all too commonly experienced. Add to that the media and propaganda campaigns that have lied, mocked, and degraded the faith and its people.

Our hope is in God and in the blessing of Imam Al-Mahdi (aj), that these attacks plunge in utter failure and Shiism comes out triumphant as it always has. "God has ordained: 'I shall surely prevail, I and My apostles.' Indeed God is all-strong, all-mighty."[3] There is no doubt that the Word of God will remain heard "so that he who perishes might perish by a

---

[2] Al-Halabi, *Taqrib Al-Ma'arif*, 188.
[3] The Holy Quran, 58:21.

manifest proof, and he who lives may live on by a manifest proof..."[4]

This hope of course must not make us negligent or lenient in our responsibility. God does not change what is within a people until they change what is within themselves. For that we must do the following:

Firstly, we must direct ourselves to God with sincere hearts and clear intentions. Let us amend and affirm our relationship with Him and be mindful of His laws and teachings. Let us befriend His friends and oppose His enemies. We must rely on Him and trust Him in good faith, and believe that He is never absent from us for even a moment.

Secondly, we must be serious in serving this noble principle, defending the faith, and safeguarding its teachings. We must support those who are upright and work closely with them. Similarly, we must refuse those who are adamantly deviant and disassociate from them. We must call onto our principles with wisdom and good counsel, just as our late scholars have done during their times of difficulty and hardship. It is from God that we seek help and success. Surely, He is the best of supporters.

---

[4] The Holy Quran, 8:42.

Words of Advice

To the believers, may God protect you all.

Hold on to your Marjaeya, as it is a symbol of honor for this school of thought. Our school of thought has distinguished itself from other schools of thought through this blessed Marjaeya. Draw yourself to it, while determining it in accordance with religious standards, with utmost sincerity and giving it due sanctity.

Be wary of the waves of doubt and denial against the fundamentals of our school of thought. As we have pointed to previously, holding firm to our principles and jurisprudence is critical. Be prudent and examine matters closely by returning to the original sources. In that, beseech the pious, sincere and prudent scholars and experts of the faith. They are worthy of trust when it comes to the religion. Remember God's words,

As for those who strive towards Us, We shall surely guide them in Our ways, and God is indeed with the virtuous.[1] Whoever is wary of God, He shall make for him a way out [of the adversities of the world and the Hereafter] and provide for him from whence he does not count upon.[2]

We ask the Almighty to keep us all steadfast in this life and the next, and to protect us from the deviation of sedition. We beseech Him from the evil of Satan, the evil of ourselves, and the demerits of our deeds. We ask that He makes us from His virtuous servants. He is indeed the most merciful, the guardian of the believers, and the best supporter.

My success is only by God, on Him I rely and to Him I turn.

And the last of our prayers is that all praise be to God, the Lord of the Worlds.

TO THE SHIA ON COEXISTENCE

The Shia community, like other communities, consists of different opinions and trends. What are your directives and advice for the Shia in living together and coexisting with one another?

Firstly, decision-making and the direction people take must be built on a few things, of course after beseeching God for success and support. There must be diligence in being aware

---

[1] The Holy Quran, 29:69.
[2] The Holy Quran, 65:2-3.

of God and what pleases Him. In addition, attention must be paid to what is best for the faith and the believers and fulfilling religious duties. In this regard, stay away from individual interests, selfish aspirations, external pressures, extremism, and blind-following. In the end, everything is for God and we are simply His servants.

Be wary of the whispers of Satan and his trickery, where he deludes to cause problems between the believers or cause a person to stray. Be vigilant of deceiving yourself into thinking you are doing something for the pleasure of God and the common good. Sweet words can be a convincing defense to one's perspective; however, if he is to reflect he may see that there are other motivations at play. Nothing escapes God.

Secondly, remove yourself from the use of violence or harshness in offering your perspective to others. Respecting people's perspectives is essential. This does not mean that you are to compromise your own position for the sake of seeing others' viewpoint. It means that you deal with others with respect, reason, tolerance, and openness. That you seek to understand the other side, lessen the tension that results in the differences present, and try to draw the similarities and commonalities that exist between you. Moreover, you allow each other to play their own role in serving the school of thought based on their own convictions.

Thirdly, there must be the utmost restraint against letting differences in opinion turn into transgressing upon each other's rights. Surely, Satan can lure people into accomplishing their goals by causing harm to those that get in their path, whether it be against another's own person physically or his family, by way of slander, bashing, or rumors – all of these acts are unacceptable to us. Indeed, infringing on the rights of a believer is one of the greatest transgressions. God says "Those who offend faithful men and women undeservedly, certainly bear the guilt of slander and flagrant sin."[3] We detailed this discussion further in our treatise to the seminarians and preachers, so this brief discussion will suffice here.

Fourthly, it should be known that having differences of opinion does not prevent us from cooperating and collaborating with one another. It does not thwart mutual regard and respect. So long as the boundaries of the school of thought are respected, which are established by unequivocal evidence and endorsed by the symbols of the school, there should be no problem.

The most important thing in setting these boundaries are the narrations of the Prophet (s) and the Imams (a). Here their teachings and perspectives are clarified and what they accept for their followers is apparent. Whoever wishes to take a position or make a decision, he should have a comprehensive background of these narrations and look deeply into them. He should examine his position based on the teachings in the narrations and assess if it is in agreement with them or not. It is not enough to have a general overview of what may be understood from the narrations or some proposed theories in that regard alone.

---

[3] The Holy Quran, 33:58.

Moreover, if a person's position goes against what is established in the faith, or moves away from it in the name of reform or renewal or as an attempt to become closer to those
outside of the school of thought – that is indeed a form of
deviation that we reject. People must not accept this sort of
direction; rather, they should stand against it and refuse to
cooperate with it. This is to protect the body of this true
school of thought, its creed, and its character from being corrupted or tainted.

To work with such people – as they affiliate themselves with
the school of thought and impose themselves on it – would
be to make way for them and validate their deviation in the
name of ijtihad and perspective. The true teachings, the con-
fines, and the fundamentals of the school of thought would
be at risk of being lost when such accommodations are made.

We seek God's blessings, support, and protection against deviance after having been guided – surely, He is the best guardian.

CREATING A STRONGER BOND BETWEEN SEMINARY AND UNIVERSITY STUDENTS

*We have noticed that in some communities there is
discongruity between the seminary students and the
university students. What is your advice to bring
them closer together?*

The students of both types of educational institutions have to make it a priority to engage in dialogue and coordinate with one another for the purpose of exchange of knowledge and experiences. They both will benefit culturally and religiously, and the faith that unites them will grow stronger.

When the seminary students open up to the university students, they are fulfilling their role of delivering the message of the faith. This is true especially considering that university students are many in number and are well rounded intellectually and culturally. Likewise, when the university students open up to the seminary students, they are able to learn more about their religion and share their own knowledge with their counterparts.

They are capable of spreading their knowledge and information to a great number of people, especially the new generations. Raising the youth with a focus on education is a great service to the faith. Those who are educating will see success for themselves and reap great rewards from their work. Dialogue, discourse, and openness between these groups will be the stepping stones to help propagate the true teachings of the faith on a global scale. It is through dialogue that understanding and awareness are achieved. Through this dialogue these students can be putting forth the greatest service to our sacred teachings, our faith, and humanity. Ultimately, they will fulfill their duty toward God and obtain His clemency, care, and support.

Yes, everyone should acknowledge the deep responsibility they have towards their faith and its teachings. They must make sure that they pay attention to receiving their religious teachings from the proper original sources – the Holy Book and the noble traditions of the Prophet (s) and his family (a). They must do so with due diligence while seeking the help of pious, trustworthy, and prudent scholars and experts.

After that, they are to present the religious teachings in its true form and within its set limitations. They are to do this in trust and with sincerity. Similarly, they should distance themselves from changing or diluting the teachings of the faith in any which way. Students should present the teachings of the faith with pride, honor, and high spirits. They should not be timid, apologetic, or overwhelmed.

Many writers and commentators have presented much of the Islamic teachings in addressing contemporary issues of life by diluting and modifying the teachings. Rather, some have completely distorted and deformed the teachings in their presentations to better suit contemporary theories and understandings that are adopted by influential modern societies.

Some have gone to the extent of denying some of the truths of Islam. They've attempted to strip Islam away from such truths for their inconsistency with contemporary ideas adopted by some of today's societies. These individuals do this in two ways.

The first is by showing that the contemporary ideas or proposals are valid by religious standards, through propagating for such ideas within Islamic society. The second way is by arguing that Islam is a modern progressive religion consistent with the ideas of the time and against backwardness – the goal here being to promote the faith and its presence. The second approach, even if the goal is a noble one, does not justify distorting the truth and altering the teachings of the religion that may very well be at odds with present ideas or proposals of contemporary society.

It is an injustice to truth and Islam – the eternal religion of God and His timeless Word – to be subjugated to the whims of modern society cradled by misguided beliefs, interests, and desires. So many empty slogans have come out of these very same places to pass dubious schemes and realize their oppressive ambitions. They do not seriously examine the ramifications of such ambitions on society, as society has suffered time and time again in their faith, ethics, and livelihood as a result of their work.

In reality, those who try to whitewash Islam and its teachings only expose their own weakness and succumbing to defeatism. Perhaps they are dazzled by those they are trying to appease, or they really believe their ideas to be truth and feel inclined to submit to them.

If it is seen that there are some gaps or negativities in the faith, it would be due to one of two reasons. It may be that society has adopted views that are contradictory to that particular teaching or conclusion in Islam; thus, those who take the contradictory view will naturally look at Islam's position as backwards even if it is better and closer to truth and reality. Or, Muslims themselves have not properly implemented that particular teaching of Islam. It could be that oppressors have taken positions that caused misrepresentations of Islam – as experienced during the lifetimes of our Imams (a). The Islam that was being practiced and witnessed was incomplete and truncated. The result of their hypocrisy and contradiction in behavior was the proliferation of various misgivings and negative propaganda against Islam – all of which the faith itself is free from and is not responsible for.

Moreover, there is no excuse to attempt to justify or distort some of issues or concepts in Islam, or to disavow or attempt to evade them. They are truths and a part of the religion which God Almighty mandated. He is the Lord of this world and all creatures in it – He surely knows what is best and dictated the most perfect system.

TO RESEARCHERS, WRITERS, AND LECTURERS

Through your insight and experience, what is the advice you give for Islamic researchers, writers and lecturers?

They must focus on producing work that is beneficial for people in bringing out the truth that would otherwise be hidden, distorted, or suppressed. They can also serve by debunking false ideas or beliefs that may be widely adopted by the public. Also, they would do well by providing guidance to people in ethics and civics, and call for unity through their work. Generally, anything that will be in the benefit of Islam and Muslims should be incorporated into their work's driving purpose. Let them be message-oriented in their work and act as ambassadors of the faith, each from their unique role. They should honor the position they are in and the talents that God has gifted them with, and be thankful and appreciative for those blessings.

They should not concern themselves with producing "popular" headlines and famous products that otherwise have no true benefit, let alone are detrimental to the faith. Be wary of work that deviates from the truth, implants sedition, or causes disunity. That would be a betrayal of what they have been entrusted with in research and knowledge. It would be a transgression against our principles and our blessings.

> *Have you not regarded those who have changed God's blessing with ingratitude, and landed their people in the house of ruin?* *—hell, which they shall enter, and it is an evil abode!*[4]

Our success is only by God, on Him we rely and to Him we shall return. And the last of our prayers is that all praise be to God, the Lord of the Worlds.

---

[4] The Holy Quran, 14:28-29.

BIBLIOGRAPHY

HOLY SCRIPTURES

The Holy Quran.

OTHER WORKS

Aal Mahboubah, Ja'far. *Maadi Al-Najaf w Hadhareha.*

Al-Ameen, Muhsin. *A'yan Al-Shia.*

Al-Amili, Muhammad ibn Al-Hassan Al-Hur. *Wasa'il Al-Shia.*

Al-Ansari, Muhammad Ali. *Al-Mawsoo'a Al-Fiqhiyya Al-Muyassara.*

Al-Arbali, Ali ibn Issa. *Kashf Al-Ghumma.*

Al-Barqi, Ahmad ibn Muhammad. *Al-Mahasin.*

Al-Bukhari, Muhammad ibn Ismail. *Sahih Al-Bukhari.*

Al-Demyari, Muhammad ibn Moussa. *Hayat Al-Hayawan.*

Al-Hakeem, Muhammad Saeed. *Misbah Al-Minhaj.*

Al-Hakeem, Muhammad Saeed. *Risala Abawiya w Masai'l Tuhim Talabet Al-Hawza wal-Muballigheen.*

Al-Halabi, Taqi ibn Najm. *Taqrib Al-Ma'arif.*

Al-Khalili, Ja'far. *Mawsoo'at Al-'Atabat Al-Muqaddasa Qism Al-Najaf Al-Ashraf.*

Al-Khaqani, Ali. *Shu'ara Al-Ghari.*

Al-Kulayni, Muhammad ibn Yaqoub. *Al-Kafi.*

Al-Majlisi, Muhammad Baqir. *Bihar Al-Anwar.*

Al-Mufid, Muhammad ibn Muhammad ibn Al-Nu'maan. *Al-Irshaad.*

Al-Mutazili, Ibn Abi Al-Hadeed. *Sharh Nahjul Balagha.*

Al-Qayrawani, Al-Hassan ibn Rasheeq. *Al-'Umda.*

Al-Radi, Muhammad ibn Al-Hussain. *Nahjul Balagha.*

Al-Sadouq, Muhammad ibn Ali. *'Uyoun Akhbar Al-Rida.*

Al-Sadouq, Muhammad ibn Ali. *Al-Khissal.*

Al-Sadouq, Muhammad ibn Ali. *Kamal Al-Deen.*

Al-Tabrasi, Al-Fadl ibn Al-Hassan. *I'lam Al-Wara bi-A'lam Al-Huda.*

Al-Tehrani, Agha Bozorg. *Nuqaba' Al-Bashar.*

Al-Toussi, Muhammad ibn Al-Hassan. *Al-Ghayba.*

Al-Toussi, Muhammad ibn Al-Hassan. *Ikhtiyar Ma'rifet Al-Rijal.*

Al-Wardi, Ali. *Lamahat Ijtima'iya min Tarikh Al-Iraq Al-Hadeeth.*

Hirzeddine, Muhammad. *Ma'arif Al-Rijal.*

Majallat Al-Daleel.

Shawket, Naji. *Al-Thikrayat.*